# AN AFFIRMATION

# JOURNEY

## FOR CAREGIVING PARENTS

## ASHLEY CABRERA

Published by Hemingway Publishers

Cover design by Hemingway Publishers

ISBN: Printed in the United States

# Dedication

*This book is dedicated to all parents of kids with medical conditions.*

# Table of Contents

# Disclaimer

I am not a licensed medical professional. The ideas presented in this book are derived from my personal experiences. It is always advisable to consult a qualified medical professional for medical advice and care.

# Preface

As a parent of two kids with rare and pressing medical needs, I faced difficulty finding support. Not many people in my every-day life could relate to my experience of taking my kids to multiple therapy appointments, keeping track of their food consumption and weight, and scheduling specialist appointments and surgeries in between. I once reached out to one of my kid's doctors about feeling overwhelmed, and she referred me to a social worker. Although the social worker had some good ideas, I still felt like I had nowhere to turn for the support I so badly needed. Taking care of children with health needs and concerns can be isolating and exhausting. I decided to write this book to let others know that they are not alone in their medical journeys with their children. I want to remind parents that you are strong and resilient, and so are your children. Yes, days can be draining and cause self-doubt and second-guessing, but you are on a wonderful expedition to take care of your precious kids, along with many others who are thinking and feeling the same way as you.

# Part 1

# Our Story

I am the oldest of five sisters. During our childhood, my younger siblings and I were relatively healthy. We would occasionally catch common illnesses, but nothing too serious. I always assumed that if I ever had children, their health stories would be similar to mine, but little did I know that would not be the case. If you're reading this, I imagine you're also experiencing a different health journey with your child.

My first daughter was born four years into my marriage in 2016. My pregnancy was normal until the delivery. Although my water broke, I didn't dilate at all, so she was delivered via C-section at full term. She was wonderful and perfect! Our first born daughter. But, right off the bat, we noticed a few concerns. She would spend a lot of the day crying. She was very constipated, and the doctor instructed us to do enemas to help her have bowel movements and relieve her discomfort. Not only did she struggle with these issues, but my body didn't make enough milk, so she was formula-fed and struggled with acid reflux. Many suggested colic, while others believed she would grow out of it. We tried various formulas until we found one that worked for her tummy. We even participated in a formula study through her pediatrician's office. Even though I was 24, people thought I was younger, and many assumed I was a teen mom. As a result, most doctors blew me off, and the first few months of being a mom were rough. Right before she turned one, our daughter started randomly spiking high fevers. These fevers were higher than what a young baby should have, so we took her to urgent care multiple times. They would run every test that was needed, with all results coming back normal – no ear infection, no strep, no bladder infection, or anything. After multiple instances of these episodes, they eventually stopped. We believed it was just a phase and that she had caught a few bugs when she was younger.

When Aliya was around two years old, she began to develop sores on her lips and chin. Her doctor initially diagnosed her with impetigo and prescribed antibiotics, which seemed to heal the sores. However, the sores kept reappearing after a week or two of being off the medication. Eventually, one of the doctors decided to take a swab to see what was causing the sores. We were very surprised when it came back showing that the sores were not impetigo but cold sores caused by the herpes virus. This newfound knowledge was astonishing because viruses don't respond to antibiotics like the sores did.

As time went on, Aliya began to experience other concerning symptoms like tummy aches, joint pain, and hair loss. On some days, she wasn't up to playing with her friends at recess. More than once, she was so unwell that she just wanted to sit with her teacher at daycare, which was so unlike her personality. If you looked at her, it looked like she had cut her hair with scissors, but she hadn't. My husband and I took her to every possible specialist that might have an answer for us. We saw an endocrinologist, a sleep doctor, a gastroenterologist, a functional medicine doctor, and more. We lived in a small town in Montana, and it was hours of driving to reach multiple of these specialists. We got our hopes up at each appointment. Then, the doctors would run their tests, and all results would come back normal. No one had any idea about what was causing our little one's debilitating issues. One doctor suggested a special diet that excluded soy, dairy, gluten, and other foods, but it didn't seem to make much of a difference.

Desperate to find answers, I reached out to the Mayo Clinic in Arizona and was able to secure an appointment a month later. I was shocked that we were scheduled at an elite medical facility - a place where people can get answers that most places are unable to give. I didn't know if we could afford to take Aliya there, but I was desperate to find out why my daughter was so sick on a regular basis.

We set up a GoFundMe campaign, and with the help of our community, we were able to travel to Arizona in November 2019. At first, we met with a dermatologist who took a hair sample and sent it off for testing. He also scheduled appointments with an allergist/immunologist and a geneticist. After all tests, it was determined that Aliya's immune system was functioning correctly, and the hair sample test returned normal results. The geneticist then suggested running a Whole Exome Sequencing (WES) on my husband, Aliya, and me. In 2019, we were told we would have our WES results in about four months. We returned back to Montana without any definitive answers. Finally, about four months later, upon receiving the results, the geneticist revealed that our daughter's test results were positive for Familial Cold Autoinflammatory Syndrome Type 2, a condition that results in the body having an autoimmune-like response to sensing cold. It can cause stomach issues, sores, fevers, and much more. The results showed that it was inherited from her dad, even though he had never shown any symptoms. However, the geneticist believed that this was not what was causing Aliya's health problems, as it was believed at that time that you would only experience symptoms if the parent who passed on the condition had shown symptoms. Since Dad had never experienced symptoms, the geneticist was fairly sure that this condition was not what was causing Aliya's health concerns. At this time, I was feeling both frustrated and confused. Aliya's symptoms seemed to match this diagnosis, which also explained why she had frequent high fevers as a young baby, yet the doctor told us this condition probably wasn't the cause of her symptoms.

Later that year, we moved our family to Texas due to a job change. When we were getting referrals for specialist appointments for Aliya at her primary care doctor's office, they suggested that we should send her to see another geneticist. Initially, I didn't understand the point of it since we had already been told that this condition was not the cause of Aliya's problems, as her dad didn't have any symptoms. Despite my reservations, we decided to meet with the geneticist. As I learned later, the field of genetics is continuously evolving. Since we had received the original test results from the geneticist, doctors discovered that some people with the genetic condition don't show any symptoms, while others do. The pediatric geneticist in Texas diagnosed our daughter with Familial Cold Autoinflammatory Syndrome Type 2 (FCAS) and referred us to allergy/immunology, along with rheumatology - two specialties that could treat her condition with medication.

Not only did Aliya struggle with a genetic condition, but she also had some sensory processing issues and fine motor difficulties. After experiencing a traumatic incident at daycare, we enrolled her in play therapy. After a few sessions, the play therapist suggested having an occupational therapy evaluation. At this point, I had no idea what occupational therapy was. I thought it was a form of therapy to help people become successful at work. Why did my two-year-old daughter need assistance to function at a workplace? Despite my confusion, we got our pediatrician to write an order for an evaluation, and that was when I was introduced to occupational therapy. I filled out a questionnaire, and the therapist played with Aliya. At the end of the appointment, the therapist told us that Aliya would qualify for services.

During the evaluation, Aliya did not want anything dirty on her hands, and playing with shaving cream scared her. She also had many other sensory-seeking behaviors, and things finally started to make sense. As a former elementary school teacher, I knew that many of the behaviors I was seeing in my daughter were not "normal." However, I did not know this realm of the medical field.

My little girl who would come and "hug" others, which felt like being strangled repeatedly, had no care for safety, had so much energy, and was always seeking more input, would jump into the pool with no one around and couldn't swim, and so much more, was struggling with the ability to process sensory information. Fine motor skills were also difficult for her, so the therapist worked on playing games that developed these skills. It was amazing to see the transformation and difference these appointments made for us. I was able to see my daughter in a new light and began to understand her world better. She was able to practice things that were harder for her in a play-based setting while having fun, an added bonus.

After the birth of Aliya, we experienced three consecutive lost pregnancies. The beginning of my fifth pregnancy also happened to be at the same time as Aliya's appointment at Mayo Clinic. More medical questions arose, this time for our second baby. Due to my history of ectopic pregnancies and miscarriages, I needed to receive immediate medical attention, beginning with HCG blood tests. After a couple of tests, my doctor informed me that my levels weren't increasing as they should, and it seemed like I was going to lose this pregnancy as well. The doctor was worried that it might be ectopic and scheduled an ultrasound appointment for me while we were in

Arizona visiting the Mayo Clinic. When we went for the ultrasound, they saw a regular pregnancy, not an ectopic one.

Nonetheless, after several bleeding scares, I went to my OB appointment. He performed an ultrasound, and surprisingly, he said that our baby was still healthy and had a heartbeat. Our baby girl was ok! I can't tell you the feeling of relief that came from this knowledge. A couple more months into the pregnancy, and I was sure this baby was trying to karate kick her way out of me. She was constantly in motion. A few months later, during one of my visits, the doctor informed me that my blood pressure was a little high and advised me to keep monitoring it. Our baby girl was expected to arrive in the middle of July, but she had other plans and was going to teach us quickly that she was in charge. We commemorated Aliya's birthday in May with a Covid-style celebration because it was 2020 and social distancing was new and enforced.

When I look back at the photos, I can see that I was very swollen at her party. In the following week, I felt unwell and kept monitoring my blood pressure, which continued to rise. I consulted my OB, who suggested that I relax at home. On Friday, still concerned after resting didn't improve my blood pressure numbers, I went to see my primary care doctor to ensure everything was alright. However, my blood pressure was dangerously high, and the doctor advised me to go to the hospital's labor and delivery unit. I arrived late in the afternoon, got a room and medication, but didn't see my doctor until the following day. He informed me that I had severe preeclampsia and would have to stay in the hospital until delivery. Our baby girl was not due for another two months, and we hadn't picked out a name for her yet.

On Sunday, the nurse told me that I was doing well and might get to go home, but the doctor repeated that I had to stay in the hospital until delivery. This news was tough because Aliya wasn't allowed in the hospital at all due to Covid. Saturday, Sunday, and Monday were pretty normal days health-wise. Aliya and my husband, JonCarlo, came on walks with me outside the hospital, and we had multiple picnics together. Monday night, I had an episode of high blood pressure. Though the nurses kept telling me to relax, I knew something was wrong. The next morning, the doctor informed me of the possibility of having our baby in the NICU due to premature birth, which felt surreal.

On Tuesday night, I had another episode of high blood pressure, and the doctor warned me I had two strikes; the next one would be the last. He talked me through what an emergency C-section would look like and had the NICU staff come and talk with me. On Wednesday evening, I told my nurse that I had a terrible headache. She quickly called the doctor, who then decided that it was strike three….time for an emergency C-section.

Our baby girl was born weighing only 3lbs and 5oz and was immediately taken to the neonatal intensive care unit (NICU). Due to Covid restrictions, only one parent was allowed to be with her at a time, so my husband and I took turns. Despite her premature birth, our baby was relatively healthy and only required bilirubin lights and a short time on the CPAP machine. However, she needed more time to develop and grow in a hospital environment and was admitted. Interestingly, she seemed happy to be in the world outside the womb, and we couldn't help but wonder if she thought she was missing out on something while in my tummy. Little did she know, the pandemic had shut down the entire world, and she was missing out on very little.

On the second day of her life, we finally agreed on a name for her, Adalie. The doctor initially predicted that she would only spend a few weeks in the NICU, and we planned on her being able to come home at about 36 weeks. But at 36 weeks, she still wasn't exhibiting the right feeding cues, and the doctor wouldn't let us feed her by mouth (she received food through an NG tube down her nose, which she hated) until she showed us she was ready. We continued to visit her and hoped that she would be able to come home soon.

Something that is such an ordinary skill for most babies and people, in general, was very difficult for our baby. I had never heard of a baby having to stay in the NICU because they wouldn't and couldn't eat the necessary amount of calories to survive. Adalie finally took her first bottle from my husband, which killed me as a mom; I wanted to be the one who fed her first! Despite trying different nipple sizes and formulas, Adalie still wasn't eating adequately. The doctors suggested that it might be time to look for reasons; most babies her age were able to make progress with eating, but Adalie wasn't.

We started trying to get answers with a swallow study, which showed she aspirated when she got tired while she was eating. (I learned that aspirating meant she let the milk she was drinking into her lungs.) It also showed that she had a decent amount of reflux. We put her on medication for the reflux, but she still didn't make much progress. Finally, an ENT came and did a scope down her throat. He and the speech therapist proceeded to tell us that Adalie's reflux was extremely bad; her throat was red and blistered. No wonder she didn't want to eat! Every time she ate, it was causing her a TON of pain. We had no idea because she wasn't a fussy baby.

After trying all the tricks and strategies to try and get her reflux controlled, including sleeping on a prescription wedge from the pharmacy, nothing was working, and we were desperate to bring Adalie home and let her meet her sister Aliya. The next option was a partial fundoplication (twisting the stomach a little bit to make it harder for the food to come back up) and a G-tube (feeding tube) so that she could get the necessary calories at home and not have to stay in the NICU. She had the surgery, and five days later, she got to come home! Holy moly! The amount of things we had to learn before she could come home. We had to learn the different parts of a G-tube, the pump, and how to give medication through her button. We had to connect with a medical supply company and home nurse who would provide us with the supplies and at-home training needed to give Adalie the nutrients and medication her body needed!

We got home the first night and tried to follow the procedures they taught us in the NICU. Adalie was allowed to eat as much as she wanted by mouth, and then she got the remainder of her calories through continuous feeds with the G-Tube. The NICU had a pre-made formula, which was already in liquid form. The liquid kind wasn't sold in stores, but they told us the powdered version of the formula was the same. That first night, we quickly learned that the powdered version of the formula was NOT the same. We tried mixing it with hot, warm, and cold water. No matter how we mixed the formula, we couldn't get anything to come out of the bottle nipple. At one point, my husband even tried to drink the milk through the bottle so that he could see what was causing the problem, but he couldn't get any milk to come out either. At that point, we called the NICU, which was an hour away from our house, and told them that we needed a little bit of premade formula to tide us over until Amazon could drop off a shipment at our house. We were one of the first to inform them that the liquid and powdered formulas were not created equally. My husband left late that night, drove to the NICU, and got a small supply of the liquid form. Crisis averted!

The following day, Adalie had a follow-up appointment with her pediatrician. As a new parent, I was still getting the hang of the G-tube and continuous feeding. We secured Adalie in her car seat and proceeded inside the doctor's office. I kept her in her car seat until the nurse arrived. At that moment, I accidentally forgot that Adalie was attached to a feeding tube. I pulled her out as I would have done with Aliya, my other child. While pulling her out, I accidentally pulled the G-tube out too. It hadn't even been a week since her surgery, and the site was still sore. Milk from the pump sprayed all over the floor, making it look like she had thrown up. The nurse was in shock and ran to get the doctor. I felt like I had failed as a parent.

The pediatrician was just as astonished when he came in! Fortunately, there was a pediatric gastroenterologist in the same office, the kind of doctor who knows how to deal with G-tubes. She hurried to her office to get the necessary items, like Vaseline, that would help the button slide back into Adalie's tummy. (I forgot to mention that we were informed from the start that the G-tube site was like an ear piercing. It would close rapidly, so if the button ever came out, we needed to rush to put it back in.)

Well, let's just say that Adalie's first regular trip to the pediatrician's office didn't go as planned. Because she hadn't even been out of surgery for a week, they sent us to the hospital for imaging to ensure that the doctor had correctly replaced the button. Fortunately, we discovered that it was in the right spot, and we were able to return home. Shortly after leaving the NICU, our family made a big move and relocated from Montana to Texas. We thought Adalie's health story could only improve from her NICU discharge, but little did we know that Adalie had some other health surprises coming in our future.

When we arrived in Texas, we had a difficult time getting our daughters enrolled in Medicaid due to the COVID-19 situation. We had been living in Montana, but my husband's company declared bankruptcy, leaving us without insurance. We needed various medical supplies, including replacement buttons, tubing, syringes, and a pump, but getting them without insurance was close to impossible. However, the "squeaky wheel gets the grease," and after repeatedly bugging people, we finally got in touch with someone in charge who helped us get through the Medicaid red tape. Shortly after, our daughters were covered by insurance.

Finding a good pediatrician in Texas was also challenging. While we came across several good ones, some of them had procedures that didn't work for us or long wait lists for new patients. We finally found a pediatrician that we liked after hearing great things about her and quickly booked an appointment. However, when we got there, she informed us that she didn't accept our insurance despite being listed as a preferred provider on our insurance company's website. During the visit, she also informed us that our daughter's head wasn't developing properly and referred us to a place that made helmets for young children.

At first, we didn't understand the importance of head shape, but we wanted to ensure that our daughter received all the medical care she needed. After an initial assessment, we found out that our daughter had plagiocephaly and needed a helmet. While we originally thought this was a cosmetic fix, we learned that it could prevent ear infections and other issues in children. The whole process of getting the helmet was time-consuming and expensive. Our insurance didn't cover it, and even though the company gave us a "special out-of-pocket" price, it was still pricey.

I remember being very reluctant to add one more thing to our routine. We already had a G-tube button site to clean and maintain and the tubes and syringes to wash, and I already felt like I was maxed out. To be honest, we didn't have Adalie wear the helmet for several days after we got it. I needed time to wrap my head around the daily helmet process. But, after having a few days to prepare mentally, we started using the helmet. Thankfully, Adalie responded to the helmet treatment quickly, and we were surprised when, at her six-week follow-up, they told us she was ready to graduate from wearing it! We had survived and could cross the helmet off our to-do list!

During one of Adalie's well-child check-ups, at around 18 months of age, the pediatrician informed us that although she was doing well, she was not growing or gaining weight as expected. As a result, he referred us to a geneticist. Fortunately, we were somewhat familiar with the process because our daughter Aliya had been diagnosed by a geneticist a few years earlier. After all the test results came back normal, the geneticist was still able to diagnose Adalie clinically with Russell Silver Syndrome. We learned that almost half of people with this disorder are diagnosed clinically because genetic testing doesn't always show the disorder is present.

Initially, we thought this syndrome would only affect Adalie's size, but we would soon learn that it had other complications as well. The geneticist informed us that Adalie qualified for growth hormone, so we began the process of getting insurance approval with the help of an endocrinologist. The specialist conducted the necessary labs, and all her levels were normal. The endocrinologist informed us that the insurance company might have difficulty approving the medication because of the normal lab work. If the medication was not approved by the insurance, they would need to conduct a stimulation test on Adalie to prove that she had a growth hormone issue. Not surprisingly, the insurance company rejected the growth hormone therapy. While we were waiting for the stimulation test appointment, the geneticist contacted us again and told us about another patient with Russell Silver Syndrome. She told us they had found a good endocrinologist in the Dallas area and offered to write a referral if we were interested. We decided to go in that direction, particularly after learning that the stimulation test had a 50-50 chance of proving that our daughter needed growth hormone.

We went to Dallas for our daughter's first visit to the new endocrinologist. The doctor agreed that she qualified for growth hormone and requested that our insurance pay for it. However, the insurance denied the request a second time. But, instead of giving up, the doctor wrote a letter to the insurance company asking for a non-biased, third-party review. He sent a copy of the letter to us, and we were impressed! He was going to bat for Adalie. The other endocrinologist gave up after the first insurance denial, but this doctor sent over evidence and medical records to prove that Adalie did qualify for growth hormone. After several months, the third-party reviewer disagreed with the insurance company's original decision, and growth hormone was approved for our daughter.

When we arrived in Texas, we needed a pediatric gastroenterologist due to Adalie having a G-tube. Most gastroenterologists had a long waitlist, and we couldn't wait that long to get a prescription for our daughter's specialty formula and feeding tube supplies. Finally, someone recommended Dr. D., and we were able to get an appointment quickly. At first, we really liked Dr. D. He paid attention to our kiddo and made her feel special. He would let her borrow his pen to color and would talk her through everything. He was the doctor we needed when we first arrived in Texas. He was very concerned about her lack of weight gain and growth. At every appointment, he told us we needed to increase the volume of food or the caloric value of the formula. This routine was so stressful! I'm not sure if anyone else has ever been in this situation, but it's impossible to will a child to gain weight. At every appointment, I held my breath, hoping that my daughter would have gained enough weight so that we could start talking about weaning off the feeding tube. Initially, when it was inserted during her NICU stay, we were told that most kids in her situation could get their feeding tubes out within six months to a year. However, we reached the six month mark and kept having to increase feed volume and/or calories. Then, we reached the year mark and still had to increase feed volume and/or calories. We met at the two-year mark, and the doctor continued to tell us she needed more calories because she wasn't gaining weight appropriately. (In fairness, he kept prescribing more feeding volume before we had her Russell Silver diagnosis, which explained her lack of growth and weight gain.)

At this point, I started to look for another gastroenterologist for a second opinion. A couple of times on our local mom's page, other parents asked for recommendations for gastroenterologists.

The same name kept coming up, a Doctor M. So I called to get an appointment. However, I was told that we wouldn't be able to make an appointment because he was a "partner" with her current gastroenterologist (Dr. D.), and that would be one doctor "stealing" another's patients. I couldn't understand how requesting to switch doctors had anything to do with a provider taking another provider's patients. The office told me to wait for a while and that maybe we could switch if enough time had passed. After a month, I called and requested an appointment again. They told me that in order to switch providers, I would have to wait for six months and not see Dr. D. during that time.

So, to jump through their hoops, we saw a different gastroenterologist at a completely separate practice for six months while we waited to get into Dr. M. Once we had passed the six month time requirement, I called and requested an appointment again. At this point, they told me that Dr. M. would have to ask Dr. D. if it was okay for him to see his patient and transfer care. I didn't realize getting the doctor we wanted for our daughter would be such a hassle. When I called back to check on the status of my request, they told me that Dr. D. had approved Dr. M. to see my daughter.

It was finally time for Adalie's first appointment with the new gastroenterologist. We went in, and to our surprise, he informed us that he didn't believe she needed her G-tube feeds anymore. While she had no oral food restrictions (except for self-imposed ones), she did have a genetic condition that caused her to be shorter and have slower weight gain. He immediately developed a plan to gradually decrease her feed volumes over the course of a month. After that month, we returned for a weigh-in to make sure she hadn't lost a bunch of weight. We were elated to find out that she had maintained the needed weight.

The next challenge was to take her off nighttime feeds entirely and transition her medication to oral administration (she has a sensory aversion to thick, white liquids). We spent the month working on giving her medication by mouth. At the next visit, the doctor asked if we felt comfortable removing the button for the tube feedings! We said yes!

Our girlie was only supposed to have the G-tube until she was six months to one year old, but it wasn't removed until she was almost three years old. I'm so glad I persisted and waited to see this new doctor. There were times of discouragement, and I questioned if the wait and effort were worth it. However, looking back, I'm incredibly grateful I trusted my initial instincts. With over a year of consistent weekly feeding therapy and occupational therapy to address her sensory aversions and developmental delays, we finally achieved our goal!

When Adalie was first diagnosed with Russell-Silver Syndrome, her pediatrician and I initially thought it was mainly a growth/weight gain disorder. Little did we know, it involved more than that, and we're still discovering all of its implications for Adalie.

At just one year old, Adalie came down with a really bad case of vomiting and diarrhea. It got so bad she couldn't keep anything down, not even her G-tube feeds. We rushed her to the emergency room, where she was diagnosed with a C. diff infection. She stayed in the hospital for several nights until she was well enough to come home.

Around the same age (around one), Adalie started getting ear infections almost monthly. After the third one, we saw an ear, nose, and throat (ENT) doctor who scheduled her for ear tube surgery. The surgery definitely helped – Adalie had fewer ear infections. After the ear tubes were put in, Adalie started getting what the doctors initially called "sinus" infections about every month. (I put sinus in quotes because the doctors ordering the antibiotics called it a sinus infection, while the ENT doctors clarified that little kids don't usually get sinus infections like adults, and the issue most likely was her adenoids.) She would get thick discharge out of her nose and a gross cough that wouldn't go away without antibiotics. They did imaging and found that her adenoids were enlarged. They removed her adenoids, but unfortunately, the "sinus" infections continued.

Next, we took Adalie to an allergist/immunologist who did some basic immune system tests. They found that she hadn't responded well to one of her childhood vaccines. They scheduled her for a booster of a more comprehensive vaccine, and after retesting her antibody levels, we saw some improvement, but not enough to completely stop the sinus infections. So, our allergist/immunologist decided to start Adalie on an antibody replacement medication.

At first, we thought the new medication was an injection like the growth hormone. We were surprised to learn it was an hour-long infusion done at home, with me administering it after training. Needless to say, I was nervous. During the training session, the pump and tubing malfunctioned. Thankfully, the nurse helped troubleshoot and ordered new equipment. I took detailed notes, hoping to manage the infusion myself next time.

The notes were helpful, but the first few times I administered the infusion alone, I felt sick. It felt like I was purposefully torturing my child. (A three-year-old doesn't understand biweekly infusions into her stomach.) Yes, even though I knew it was a doctor-prescribed medication and that it was given to help her, it took a while to feel comfortable with the process.

One positive outcome: after several infusions, Adalie caught a cold, an average virus. Before she was on antibody replacement medication, this average cold would lead to a sinus or ear infection. But miraculously, with the medication, her body fought it off – no antibiotics needed! By this point, I was finally more at ease giving her the infusions. Don't get me wrong, it's not exactly fun for either of us. But the results are incredible and worth the initial struggle.

In addition to all of these parts of Adalie's story, snoring led to a sleep study that revealed central apnea (where the brain forgets to tell you to breathe while sleeping). The sleep specialist then ordered an MRI, which came back normal. Yet, Adalie's sleep struggles persisted. After conducting further research, I found another sleep specialist. We explained that Adalie's adenoid removal surgery was supposed to alleviate her sleep apnea, but it seemed like she was still struggling with the condition. The new doctor scheduled us for another sleep study, and the results revealed that Adalie was experiencing obstructive sleep apnea episodes. The doctor advised us to consider getting her tonsils removed to increase the size of her airway and reduce the risk of tissue collapse while she was sleeping. However, the ENT was hesitant to take her tonsils out because they weren't enlarged. He suggested waiting a few months to see if the sleeping issues persisted before scheduling the surgery. After a month, Adalie was still waking up multiple times during the night, so we contacted the doctor again and pleaded with him to schedule the tonsillectomy. Little did we know that this surgery would have both positive and negative outcomes.

After discovering that one of the symptoms that usually arises with Russell Silver Syndrome was hypoglycemia, the doctor decided to admit Adalie overnight before her tonsil surgery. He wanted her to receive an IV with sugar to prevent hypoglycemia that could easily occur with pre-surgery fasting. However, Adalie was not happy about staying an extra night in the hospital.

The next morning, they woke us up bright and early, and she had her tonsillectomy. The doctor suggested that she stay another night to make sure she started consuming food or at the least, drinking fluids. Adalie, being the strong-willed person that she is, decided that she didn't want to eat or drink. Both of those things hurt after having a tonsillectomy, and she didn't want to be in more pain. On the evening of the day she had surgery, she wasn't doing very well. Out of nowhere, she started vomiting blood. The nurses called the doctor immediately. She was taken back to the operating room to control the bleeding. Everything went well with the surgery, and the surgeon came out and told me she was doing well. About five minutes later, he rushed out and told me that after removing the breathing tube, she started to bleed again and had to be re-sedated. Fortunately, they finally got the bleeding under control, and Adalie returned to her room. The hope was that we could go home the next day. But Adalie had her own plans. She wanted to go home badly and hated being in the hospital but continued to refuse to eat or drink. When the doctor would try to disconnect her from the sugar

IV, Adalie would become hypoglycemic, showing that she wasn't stable without the IV. This knowledge meant we couldn't leave the hospital. After 11 days in the hospital, Adalie finally started showing some interest in food and drink. We decided to take her home and let her try eating and drinking there. She finally started eating and drinking. Holy trauma for her and her family!

Looking back, now that we have their diagnoses, everything we experienced for years makes sense, but in the middle of getting diagnoses and before, life was crazy and unpredictable. We wondered if life would always be so random and require immediately going from solving one problem to the next without any type of break. For our family, getting diagnoses has been a game-changer in streamlining the girls' care and has allowed us to be able to sit back in our seats instead of always sitting on the edge, afraid for what might happen next.

# Part 2

# Helpful Tips and

# Lessons Learned

# Finances

Let's be one hundred percent honest! I understand that managing the financial aspects of having children with medical needs can be incredibly challenging. Even before having kids, my husband and I had our own health issues to deal with, resulting in ongoing medical expenses. Despite our efforts to budget and pay off debts, it's difficult when income doesn't cover both the cost of living and the medical bills.

**Insurance:**

My first piece of advice is to ALWAYS research your health insurance options. If you are purchasing from the HealthCare.gov marketplace, you will have multiple choices. You can look up specialists and primary care doctors you are already established with to make sure they are included in the plan you are considering joining. Also, check if the plan covers the medications you require. It's important to ensure that your insurance will cover the needed doctors and medications before selecting your plan from the Health Marketplace.

If you are getting insurance through an employer, there are usually multiple options available. Health insurance is not something that you learn much about before you become an adult, and it's worth noting that some people are able to survive without medical insurance. That has never, and will never be something that works for our family!

Most recently, my husband's company offered three different medical plans: a high deductible plan with a health savings account option and two more traditional plans where you pay a copay (a set amount) for general services and your deductible (another set dollar amount). Once your deductible is met, the insurance starts covering a higher percentage of your healthcare costs. In the first year that he selected health insurance, we picked the plan with the highest premium (the amount that came out of my husband's paycheck for each pay period) and lowest deductible. This plan ensured that we got more assistance from the insurance during the whole year. Instead of choosing a high deductible plan, where you have to meet your deductible before the insurance pays anything, opting for the higher premium plan meant we paid more each month out of my husband's paycheck for having insurance. Still, the insurance immediately helped out with primary care and specialist copays. We knew there was no way we would be able to afford all the medical supplies and formula that Adalie's G-tube required at 100% of the cost until we reached a deductible amount. So, at the time, it worked best for us to pay the insurance company a higher premium each month which ensured that we only had to pay for a portion of services even before we met our deductible.

Fast forward to this most recent year, when we selected our medical plan, my mom taught me a trick. She advised me to look at each plan and add the cost of the premiums (annual cost of being enrolled in the plan) to the cost of the out-of-pocket maximum. This gives us the possible total we will have to pay out-of-pocket for medical insurance and bills during the course of the insurance plan year. Upon comparing the totals this time, we found that the total amount we would pay out of pocket for medical expenses would be cheaper with the high deductible plan/health savings account plan. Although we don't want to meet the out-of-pocket maximum each year, with our family's track record, it makes more sense for us to assume that we will meet it and figure out how we can pay the least possible amount during the year for healthcare, because as you all know, it is VERY expensive.

In the past couple of years, we have picked health care plans that allow us to have a health savings account. Health savings accounts have been a GREAT asset for our family. Every month, some of my husband's paychecks are put straight into an account for medical expenses. By using this special account, it has allowed us to plan ahead for medical bills. Instead of being pushed into the negative in our monthly budget whenever we receive a medical bill, we now have money set aside that we can use to pay for them and only them. After much consideration, we decided to almost put the maximum amount of money in our HSA account for the year. With the medical costs that our family accrues, this has been an amazing option that prevents medical bills from setting us back too far financially.

We went through a period when our kids were eligible for state Medicaid. This happened after my husband lost his job due to his employer declaring bankruptcy, and our income dropped enough for us to qualify for Medicaid. I strongly recommend checking your state's income limits to see if you qualify for state Medicaid or a Medicaid waiver for kids with medical issues. State Medicaid offers many benefits, including coverage for almost all medical expenses at 100%, rides to and from appointments, reimbursement for transportation costs, and more.

After getting your insurance, always double-check to ensure that the providers you or your children are scheduled to see are in-network with your insurance company. In-network means that the doctor and the insurance company have agreed on the cost of services, and the doctor's office cannot bill you more than that agreed amount. If you visit an out-of-network doctor, you won't have the protection of your insurance determining a reasonable billing amount, and you could end up with significantly higher bills than if you had seen an in-network provider.

Always, always, always make sure to review the explanations of benefits (EOBs) that you receive from your insurance company. Compare them to the bills you get from the doctor's office to make certain that the amounts you owe match. Mistakes can happen because people work at insurance companies, and just like everyone else, they can make errors. There have been times when we didn't compare the bill and the EOB quickly enough, and we missed the insurance's appeal deadline even though a mistake had been made. Your insurance always sets a time frame for appealing or disputing their decisions, and you can find the details in your plan coverage book or in the paperwork that comes with your EOBs.

If you have the opportunity to obtain secondary insurance and it isn't a financial burden, please sign up for it. Having secondary insurance for our children was a HUGE blessing. Secondary insurance is essentially a second health insurance plan. One health insurance plan will be considered "primary" and will be the first to be billed by providers. Normally, whatever isn't paid after the primary insurance has contributed becomes your balance. However, the great thing about secondary insurance is that the remaining balance you would have owed if you only had primary insurance is now billed to the secondary insurance, and in many cases, they pay the difference. Always verify the specifics of your coverage before making decisions. During the short time that we had secondary insurance, it was amazing! All the amounts that we would normally owe were covered by the secondary insurance, and these amounts still counted toward our primary insurance's deductible. In simple terms, we could meet our deductible without paying a cent other than the monthly premiums.

Be persistent when dealing with insurance companies. We faced a problem that took about a year to resolve. I had to call the insurance company multiple times a month. Initially, it was chaotic as the agents didn't even know my plan year. Some said our insurance year was January-December, while others said it was April-March. After numerous phone calls without progress, I finally had to file a complaint with the state where we lived at the time. After the state got involved, I received an apology letter from the insurance company along with a letter explaining how the issue was resolved.

We've definitely learned from our experiences with insurance. For example, at one point, when my husband and I were both working, it seemed cheaper for him to have an individual insurance plan through his work while Aliya and I were on the insurance offered by my employer. We only looked at the price of the monthly premiums when making our decision. Although the family premium was more expensive, we didn't consider that instead of all expenses contributing to the same family deductible, my husband had his own deductible for his plan. Aliya and I had a separate one through my insurance plan. So, when my husband needed an emergency appendectomy, the expenses only went towards his insurance deductible instead of getting us closer to a family deductible total. We won't make that mistake again. It has been better for our family to be on the same insurance plan, working towards the same deductible and out-of-pocket maximum.

Please understand the meaning of the term "out-of-pocket maximum" for your plan. One year, Adalie reached our family's out-of-pocket maximum before anyone else had met their deductibles. Whenever Aliya, my husband, or I tried to visit the doctor, they would claim we owed money because we hadn't met our deductibles. This issue required multiple phone calls with the insurance company. Still, our current plan states that once our family meets the out-of-pocket maximum, everyone is covered at 100% (the insurance pays for all in-network medical costs) regardless of whether their deductible has been met or not. At this point, our out-of-pocket maximum took precedence over any deductibles. I was surprised at how many doctors' offices didn't realize that we didn't need to meet our deductible once our family's out-of-pocket maximum was met.

It's important to remember that neither the doctors' offices nor the insurance companies have a personal stake in the process. They handle their initial billing and explanation of benefits (EOBs), then move on. For instance, we received a bill where the insurance company denied the entire claim because they had requested more information from the hospital, which they never received. At this point, the insurance company had no obligation to pay because they were waiting for the required information from the hospital, and they weren't in a rush to obtain it because they didn't want to pay. The hospital also had no immediate incentive to act. Even if the insurance didn't pay, they could still bill us and collect their money. The only ones at risk in this situation were our family. Since no one else had a personal investment in this scenario, we had to put in all the effort. Despite being told by hospital and insurance workers that it shouldn't be our responsibility, we were the ones most affected by the situation. If I hadn't persistently contacted the hospital and insurance, the insurance company could have avoided paying. However, due to our persistence and attention to the bills and documents, we discovered that the insurance owed the entire balance after receiving further information from the hospital, and we owed nothing. Although it took about a year to resolve, the savings of thousands of dollars made it worthwhile to pay attention to details and make repetitive, frustrating calls to the insurance company.

**Medical Bills:**

If you have medical bills that were not covered by insurance, or if they are part of your copay or deductible, you have a couple of options.

First, you can call and ask the provider if they would be willing to offer you a pay-in-full discount. Many places will give you a percentage off your total bill if you can pay your account in full when you receive the bill.

Second, you can ask the company to allow you to set up a payment plan. However, be cautious with this option! Some medical offices will allow you to set up a low monthly payment plan as long as they can automatically charge the payment each month. Other medical offices require that the total balance be paid in full within a certain amount of time, making the monthly payment more expensive.

A major mistake we made in the early years of paying medical bills was trying to get the pay-in-full discount by putting the balance on a credit card. Medical debt doesn't collect interest. But, if you put that whole balance on the credit card, you'll end up paying more in interest than you received in the discount, a lesson we learned the hard way. So, if possible, avoid putting medical expenses on credit cards. But, if you have to, you have to. Sometimes, there isn't another way!

Another tip with medical bills: always save your out-of-pocket medical expenses receipts. If you are like our family, these generally add up to a considerable amount of money. If you have records of the amounts and are able to itemize deductions on your tax return, this process can save you money each year.

On the realistic side of things, it really stinks to know that a lot of your income is going toward medical bills. But remember, you are investing in people you love. What is more important than that?

# Finding Doctors

Finding a doctor might seem as easy as searching for the specialty on Google and choosing someone with good reviews. However, while looking at doctor's reviews can be very helpful, it's important not to rely solely on other people's reviews when choosing a doctor. As we discussed in the insurance section, not all doctors are covered by your insurance plan. So, first and foremost, you need to ensure that you are finding a doctor who is covered by your insurance. If you go to a doctor who is "not covered," you will end up paying extra, usually a significant amount more than if the provider was in-network.

Once you find a doctor with good reviews who is covered by your insurance plan, you can call and schedule an appointment. Depending on the doctor's office and your insurance, you might need a referral from your primary care doctor, essentially a letter from them stating that you need to see the specialist for reasons x, y, and z. Some insurance plans don't require a referral from a primary care doctor to see a specialist, so make sure to know the specifics of your plan.

Next, find out how soon their earliest new patient appointment is. Unfortunately, popular places often have appointment waitlists that can last for months, if not years. In both of our daughters' cases, some issues were urgent enough that I wasn't willing to wait that long. I kept looking for doctors who could get us in earlier. Many doctors have online portals now. On several apps that we have used for different providers, we are actually able to click if we would like to be put on a waitlist for a cancellation. When an appointment gets canceled, the app notifies us and asks us if this new appointment time works in our schedule. Other times, doctor's offices have told us to call back daily to check for cancellations. Several times, I have called back almost daily, which I think they were surprised about and also annoyed, but they gave me the next available appointment, which was much sooner than we were originally scheduled. As with most things in life, "The squeaky wheel gets the grease."

If you are not satisfied with the advice or treatment provided by a doctor, or if something doesn't feel right, remember that you have the right to seek a second opinion. For instance, my daughter Adalie was experiencing frequent infections and had been on antibiotics for 10 out of the last 12 months. When I took her medical and pharmacy records to a specialist, the specialist dismissed us and was quite rude! She said, "Well, Adalie, your mom seems to think you have a problem, but I just don't see it!" Despite having all the medical records to prove Adalie's chronic infections, the provider did not seem to care, possibly because many of the records were from urgent care facilities and not the prestigious clinic where she worked.

We were supposed to follow-up with this doctor in a month, but I couldn't bring myself to go back and get talked down to like that, especially when I was just looking out for the best interests of my daughter. So, we found another ENT and went to him. He asked why we didn't stick with the original doctor, and I told him how she had not validated my concerns. After examining my daughter, he proceeded to tell me that Adalie's health issues were not in my head but rather in her head (fitting because she was having chronic sinus issues).

I also sought additional opinions from different gastroenterologists, endocrinologists, and sleep doctors. I am determined to get my children the best medical care possible, and if that takes testing out multiple providers, I'm okay with that. Yes, it gets exhausting and discouraging, but now, after visiting with so many providers, I feel like both of my girls have "the dream team" of doctors.

Don't hesitate to ask your kids' doctors questions. Most of us parents don't have medical training, so there's a lot for us to learn and understand. I recommend using a doctor's online portal as much as possible if it's an option. Many doctors respond quickly to questions and concerns through their clinic's messaging portal. Some may respond more quickly to phone calls. Unfortunately, it's a learning experience with each doctor's office.

I also suggest being observant of the environment when you're at the doctor's office. For example, one clinic we visited was a teaching clinic, and nearly every visit involved interacting with a medical student. While I have no problem with students learning, at this clinic, the students would conduct an initial exam and history on their own, then leave us in the exam room while going to "talk to the doctor." We would wait for a while, and finally, the doctor and the student would return for the actual examination. This process significantly increased the appointment time; it felt like three appointments combined in one. I always left this doctor's office feeling grumpy, frustrated, and like I had wasted a lot of time. Unless I absolutely loved the doctor at this clinic, we made sure to find a doctor at a different clinic that would allow us to complete our visits more quickly.

# Anxiety, Depression, and Mental Health

To every person who takes care of someone with medical needs, know that you are not alone! I understand how utterly exhausting it can be. Not only is it exhausting sometimes, but taking care of someone else's medical needs can cause trauma in your life.

First of all, please recognize that what you're doing is both challenging and beautiful. You are making a significant impact on someone's life, even though it takes a toll on you. I personally need a good amount of sleep and don't function well without it. I realize that the time spent in waiting rooms could have been used for your hobbies, work, or anything else you prefer.

I understand that my perspective may be different due to the three lost pregnancies, but I consider my children to be my living miracles. Without medical intervention, either my kids or I or all of us would have died during the childbirth process. With that being said, I want to give my two miracles the best possible life. I have already spent a decent amount of time feeling guilty and shaming myself for all the health problems my kids have. I took care of myself and my babies during pregnancy, and yet they both have difficult health conditions that will most likely affect their whole lives. What's interesting to me is that I don't blame my parents for the autoimmune genes that were passed down to me. I know that they didn't get to choose where they came from and what genes they were given. But somehow, for me, those same thoughts have struggled to apply to me and my children. I have regularly felt guilt and shame because I couldn't give them a "normal," healthy childhood.

As a kid, I remember being carefree. My parents loved and supported me, and I enjoyed activities like piano lessons, playing outside, making friends with the neighbors, and so much more. I don't recall facing any significant challenges during my early years.

Now, as a parent, I see that my own children have already experienced numerous difficulties before the age of four. Both of my children feel anxious about going to the doctor due to the potential challenges associated with medical appointments. It could include a blood draw, a shot, a new feeding tube button, a urine sample, a catheter, a finger prick, and so much more. Poor Adalie was so traumatized that one time, as we were walking into Lowe's to get some items for our house, she said, "No, Mommy! I don't want to get a blood draw!" Every time we go to an appointment, Adalie runs through a list of things that could happen when she's at the doctor. She always asks, "Is this just a talking appointment?" (an appointment that only requires conversation and no testing or procedures.) While I was telling Adalie that Aliya was going to have surgery to repair her umbilical hernia, Adalie said, "Mom, I hope they don't give her a hand pillow." She remembered the process of getting an IV and having it strapped down to her hand so it didn't come out; she didn't want her sister to have that same experience.

Aliya started play therapy when she was about 2 ½-3 years old. The therapist immediately noted that she had a lot of medical trauma and anxiety because she would always get the baby off the shelf, along with the doctoring tools, and work on doctoring the baby.

During Adalie's neuro examination, the doctor informed me that her anxiety, particularly about medical issues, led her to create many rigid rules. After the doctor mentioned this, Adalie's inability to be flexible made perfect sense. Adalie was attempting to manage her anxiety by controlling everything she could.

When it comes to your kiddo's mental health, it's important to have them see a therapist, play therapist, attend counseling, or seek other types of treatment if you notice any signs that they may need it. One of my daughter's therapists once told me that typically, when young kids make progress in their mental health, they don't usually regress; they are generally able to maintain the progress they have made and face future challenges better equipped.

I can see how a child could easily feel depressed about their medical situation. In today's world, there is a lot of comparison, and medical issues can easily make people feel different and left out. Whether a medical condition makes a child look different, need different things, or act differently, other children quickly notice these differences. It's crucial to build your child up and focus on their strengths. When Aliya found out she needed feeding therapy, tears welled up in her eyes, and she asked, "Mom, does this mean I'm in trouble?" The answer was absolutely not! Something I have always told her from a very young age is that everyone is different, and we all have different needs. She needed to work a little extra on eating, while other people needed to spend extra time working on other skills. On the other hand, she also has strengths that other people may not have. It's important to identify your kiddo's strengths so that they don't focus solely on their differences or weaknesses.

Yes, getting mental health assistance for your kiddo may seem like another task to add to your schedule, but I have seen incredible results in Aliya from her counseling experience. She has a high pain tolerance and always likes to appear tough. These traits often made it difficult for her to express what was hurting or where, and she would tell me and doctors that everything was good when clearly her body language showed me she was in pain or discomfort. After years of working on expressing feelings, she has started to communicate her emotions and let us know when something is wrong. This progress means the world to me!

Many large clinics also have child life specialists, which are a great resource for helping kids understand their conditions and helping them relax during appointments. I was not familiar with this occupation previously but was so grateful when one specialist calmed and distracted my child before a blood draw.

This section is where it gets hard, and I've procrastinated writing it because it's a tough subject for me. Being a caregiver to children with medical needs can cause mental health issues in the caregivers themselves. To be honest, I have dealt with these mental health struggles throughout my whole caregiving process. I have sought help from a counselor for years and am still currently working with one. I also am on some medication to help with anxiety and depression. I think a big part of this is that we are trying to juggle everyday life while helping someone who needs extra help, and it is often exhausting. Everyday life doesn't just stop. For example, we had one week where there was a doctor's appointment for one of the girls or me daily. The next week, we were supposed to only have Adalie's regular OT appointment and then get a break. I was looking forward to relaxing and just doing simple things at home with my girls, like baking soda and vinegar volcanoes outside. When it got to that week that we were supposed to have a break, something urgent medically came up every day, and we ended up having appointments every day that week. Not only that, but then we had a pipe that started leaking into our yard. To cut down on costs, I had to dig a trench for the new pipe in the hot summer Texas sun. After that week, I told my husband that I needed a day to catch my breath. He's really good about taking the girls on a Saturday when I don't have anything left to give to anyone. That has been really helpful and rejuvenating for me. But, when I woke up that specific morning, Aliya couldn't walk and was in an extreme amount of abdominal pain, requiring us to spend two days in the hospital, which you probably know is not a place to catch up on sleep. Then, we ended up with specialist appointments and follow-ups during the week to see if we could get more answers as to why she had been in so much pain.

It was a constant struggle between dealing with real life and medical issues. There were days, actually a good chunk of them, when it was hard for me to get out of bed due to mental and physical exhaustion. I usually manage well when I know I have scheduled breaks to catch my breath, but those breaks keep getting delayed. This left me feeling worn down and discouraged, and I noticed that when I get too burnt out, I become angry. Not necessarily angry at anyone in particular, but angry at the relentless demands placed on me. Taking care of all your children's needs can leave you with no time to take care of yourself. Guess what? You are a person who still has needs. I've learned from personal experience that neglecting my own needs results in me being a very grumpy, fatigued, and angry mom.

Let's look at some areas of being a caregiver that can cause extra stress and anxiety.

1. Traveling to and from and keeping track of information at appointments.
2. Making decisions about what direction to proceed with your child's treatment/care.
3. Am I nervous due to my child's underlying medical conditions, or are there current symptoms urgent?
4. Do we need to go to this doctor's appointment?
5. What do the receptionists and doctors think? Sometimes, it feels like we live at the doctor's office.
6. Why is it that when we seem to get one thing figured out or solve a crisis, another one pops up in its place?
7. Is this treatment/surgery necessary, or is it causing unnecessary pain to my child?
8. Is the school going to reach out due to my child's number of medical-related absences? (even though she has a 504 plan)

As a parent or caregiver to children with medical needs, I often experience anxiety about various things, including the list above. Do any of these situations sound familiar to you? Here are a few ways I have found to help with my anxiety.

Firstly, taking a break is essential. Scheduling a day to be alone, to spend time with friends, or take the children somewhere enjoyable can be very beneficial. After a long series of medical appointments or particularly challenging ones, we try to plan something entertaining. Our girls particularly enjoy indoor playgrounds, trampoline parks, art project places, water parks, splash pads, and much more. I have discovered that setting aside a day for these types of activities is rejuvenating for all of us. It allows us to have fun together and put our medical concerns aside for a day. We get to pretend to be like regular people living a "normal" daily life.

Second, take care of yourself. My dad always reminds me that in airplane safety demonstrations, the flight attendants always tell you to put on your oxygen mask if needed before helping someone else. The same principle applies to being a caregiver. Look for self-care activities online and try to fit in several a week or one a day. Try to eat balanced meals and ensure you are getting all the food groups. Exercise is another option that can be really helpful. It can help you work out your stress and also make you feel accomplished.

Third, find an outlet or hobby. Playing the piano is something that helps me express myself while listening to music, and it helps me relax.

Fourth, set realistic expectations. Don't worry if your house doesn't get cleaned as often as you would like or isn't spotless and perfect all the time. One morning, a couple of neighbors started giving me advice on how to take care of my front flower bed. I politely explained to them that right now, I am raising children, and I don't have much time (actually no time) to worry about or take care of plants. Maybe later in my life, I'll have time to take care of plants if I want to.

Fifth, get sleep! This step is so much easier said than done but so important. I'm the type of person who struggles to function without enough sleep. I can't think, make decisions, and barely get through the day if I don't get my minimum hours of sleep. That's why I often take naps. Yes, I have naps on a regular basis because I know that without the right amount of sleep, everything becomes much more difficult. However, there are times when you can't control how much sleep you get. For example, my daughter, Adalie, struggles with sleep apnea, which causes night terrors. There are nights when I'm up with her four times. In the hospital, the constant checking on patients is good but doesn't allow for a lot of quality sleep. I do my best to get sleep when I can.

Sixth, make sure to have something to look forward to in the near future. It can be as simple as getting a candy bar or some type of treat after an appointment, going on a date with your child or significant other, planning a vacation, or a family adventure. Having these positive things to look forward to has been a game-changer for me. In fact, I notice that when I don't have anything to look forward to, that is when my mental health can struggle the most.

These are just a few strategies that have helped me manage the anxieties of caring for children with medical needs. I encourage you to reflect on your own life and identify what has been helpful for you. Incorporate these practices into your routine to create a more balanced and manageable life.

Remember, you are a good parent! You're doing your best to care for your kiddo, and while it can feel like a heavy burden, you are living it and managing it every day. Remind yourself often that being a good parent doesn't mean you won't make mistakes; it means you care for your child with love. The times when a doctor, another parent, or anyone else who works with my kiddo tells me that I am doing a good job mean the world to me. See if you can be the one who shares an encouraging message with other parents in similar situations.

# Reaching Out

There are many parents in similar situations: taking care of kids with multiple health issues while feeling burnt out and alone. One thing I would encourage you to do is to reach out to others who are in a similar situation. For example, one Sunday at church, I heard a story of a lady who sat with and spoke to another person in a waiting room. The two were able to exchange stories and just be there for each other. Now, to be completely honest, I am 100% an introvert. But hearing this story inspired me.

A few days later, I found myself sitting in the waiting room while my daughter was sedated for an MRI. As I waited, another mom came with her kiddo, and I couldn't help but overhear her conversation with the doctor. Her daughter had just undergone an endoscopy, and they discovered an issue with the feeding tube already placed in her stomach. The doctor who completed the endoscopy instructed her to go upstairs immediately to have it checked. The little girl was still groggy from the procedure, and as the doctor, nurse, and child life specialist discussed the next steps with the mom, she repeatedly insisted, "I have always gone back with my daughter for this procedure. She needs me there to comfort her! It takes a lot of us to hold her down so that this process can be completed."

The medical professionals in charge stated that she couldn't have been with her daughter for this procedure before. They explained that it was the facility's policy that only medical personnel could be present during the procedure. After pleading with the doctors and nurses to let her go back, she finally realized that no one was going to make an exception to the policy. She became emotional and made a phone call. Then, it was time for her daughter to go back to the procedure room, and the mom was left alone in the waiting room. As an introvert, my initial inclination was to sympathize with the mom but remain in my seat in silence, sending good feelings her way through the waiting room. I wasn't sure if she would even notice, but it was easier to stay put and wait for my daughter. However, on that day, inspired by the story I recently heard at church about the positive impact of reaching out to others, I decided to step out of my comfort zone. I left my seat, walked over to the mom, and hugged her. Then, I sat by her, and we shared stories. She explained that she was a single mom and that her daughter had been healthy until recently. Doctors were unsure what was causing her little girl to be sick, but she had spent a lot of time in the hospital. The mom had no family in the area and was hopeful that her mom would move nearby in the near future but also seemed unsure if this was actually feasible. This conversation was a powerful reminder that I was not alone in our medical journey with our children, and I hope that she was able to feel the same way, at least for a moment.

This tender experience will stay with me forever, and I hope the memory of it encourages me to reach out to others in similar situations. So many parents just want to be seen, and guess what? In our walk of life, we have the opportunity to make them feel noticed. A simple hello and a smile can make a big difference. Other ways to reach out include sending a text, sharing a personal story, dropping off a card or flowers, and much more. One mom was always in the OT waiting room on the same days and at the same times as our appointments, and she always made it a point to say hi to my girls and me, brightening our days.

Recently, I experienced the impact of someone reaching out to me, and she will probably never know how much of a lifesaver she was. My oldest daughter had just come home from the hospital. We thought she had appendicitis, but the doctors didn't check for it. After an overnight stay, fluids, and dextrose to increase her blood sugar, we were discharged without answers. The night before we went to the hospital, my youngest was up multiple times, needing me to rock her. Needless to say, I hadn't gotten much sleep that night. Not only was I in short supply of sleep, but the doctors never figured out what caused this extreme episode of pain in my daughter, and I was thinking of every possible test that we should run to find answers. Shortly before we left the hospital, a friend I hadn't heard from in a while randomly texted to say she missed me. I explained that we were in the hospital, that I was exhausted, and that we didn't quite know what was going on. She immediately offered to bring us dinner for the next two nights.

Normally, I would have told her that we were ok, I could make dinner, but I didn't hardly have the energy to drive home. The day she brought us dinner, every now and again, I would think to myself, "What are we having for dinner tonight? I don't have it in me to cook." Every time I worried about dinner, I remembered someone was taking care of it, which brought immense relief. What might have seemed like a small gesture to her was a significant help to me. I will never forget how much her reaching out allowed me to keep going.

Another way to reach out is to ask for help, which can be very difficult but such a blessing to your whole family. I know for a fact that we would never have made it on our own throughout this journey. When Adalie was born, the NICU was about an hour away from our home. The Ronald McDonald House wouldn't accept us because we had our older daughter, and it wasn't feasible to drive one hour to the hospital and one hour back multiple times a day. We also couldn't afford to stay in a hotel for the foreseeable future. My aunt and uncle offered to let us stay at their house, which was only about 20-30 minutes from the NICU.

At first, I didn't want to accept their offer. We would be a burden on them, we'd never be able to "pay" them back, and I would always have eyes on me; I would never be able to truly relax, cry, or feel any of the emotions I needed to feel, because I often feel the need to be tough in front of other people. Even though staying at their house wasn't the ideal situation for me, it was the best option we had available to us at that time. Looking back, I don't know how we would have made it through our NICU experience if we hadn't stayed at their house.

My aunt and cousin spent a lot of time playing with my older daughter; this whole period was very traumatic for her as well, and I spent a lot of time at the hospital. They were there for her when I couldn't be in two places at once. We would go on walks in the evening, and just being able to talk and get fresh air brought a rejuvenation of spirit. Originally, when we accepted the offer to stay at their house, my husband and I told them we could cook our own meals and pay for our own groceries. My aunt and uncle wouldn't hear of it. They insisted on cooking meals for us and sharing their groceries.

Again, this assistance was a huge blessing to my family; I wouldn't have had the energy to cook most days, and we would have ended up having a lot of fast food. Instead, we were able to eat well-balanced, home-cooked meals and dine in a family setting.

I was brought up to work hard and be self-sufficient, but our family's circumstances have not always allowed us to do so. When my husband was unemployed due to a layoff, we sought help to pay our bills. We also applied for Medicaid, SNAP, and WIC.

Before our oldest daughter was diagnosed with her genetic condition, we needed to take her to Mayo Clinic in Scottsdale, AZ. We didn't have the funds for the trip, so we started a GoFundMe campaign. The support and generosity we received were overwhelming—even those who couldn't donate helped in other ways, such as offering hotel points and more. A friend also informed me about a foundation that assists with medical expenses. We reached out to them, and they helped cover the cost of airfare.

During the Christmas season, we received a heartwarming invitation to participate in a special program organized by the same foundation that had helped with our airfare—the program aimed to cover the Christmas expenses for children from families struggling with medical costs. We signed our daughter up for the program and were amazed by the outcome. All we had to do was provide the foundation with a wish list for our daughter for Christmas. Then, in December, they organized a special Christmas celebration for families with kids who have medical needs. They treated us to a lovely dinner and a show, and at the end of the night, they presented each child with a stack of presents. Sponsors quietly stood by as each child opened a gift.

Aliya received a Barbie airplane and was so excited! This was her big-ticket item, and her face lit up. After opening the first gift, families got to take the rest of the presents home to save for Christmas day. I absolutely love the Christmas season, and I will never forget the love, joy, and hope that we felt due to the foundation's Christmas program. It helped us keep going and not be discouraged about the holidays because we knew that even if we couldn't buy Aliya another present, another thoughtful donor had taken care of her Christmas for us! She was still going to have a magical day!

# Making and Keepsake Memories

Another thing that has been helpful in keeping us going on this medical journey is finding ways to make and preserve memories. In difficult times, it's important to be able to look back and remember what a great day you had in the past!

Probably in large part due to all of the medical tests, procedures, surgeries, etc., my girls also struggle with anxiety. To help them cope, we try to do something positive after challenging visits, procedures, etc. For example, after Adalie's blood draws, which make her extremely nervous, we let her pick out a candy bar from the nearest store. Aliya was scared to go potty into a hat. After she gave Mayo Clinic a urine sample, we went to Walmart and let her pick out a toy. I'm not suggesting that you purchase something after every blood draw, test, or procedure, but I have found it helpful to notice what my kids are most anxious about and have something positive for them to look forward to after they have been brave.

Other times, we have had to take longer trips to see specialists. Besides having to fly to Arizona, we drive to see a specialist that is about four hours away. Sometimes, I dread this trip because it is too long for our family to do a "there and back trip" on the same day, but it is also exhausting to do a quick trip there and a quick trip back the next day. So, we've tried to make some memories in the process. Our girls generally love being able to watch shows during long car rides. But, one of the last times we went to see this specialist, I found a couple of car games to play. One of them was a set of scavenger hunt cards for car rides. Aliya would pull out several cards and list things that we were supposed to look for while we were driving. After finding one, we would discard that card and add another item to our list of things to find.

Another game provided us with different challenges. Our family currently does better working collaboratively instead of competitively, so we tweaked the game a little bit so we could work together.

Some of the challenges included singing a song, giving a massage, thinking back on other memories, and more. These games were such a fun twist to our car ride.

Also, the last time we drove to the specialist, we saw an advertisement for a museum on the way. We randomly decided to stop. The museum happened to be a prison museum, and after walking through, I realized that it wasn't the best place for young children; there was an electric chair on display, different tools that prisoners used, and more. But, in the lot nearby, there was a memorial for correction workers and a bell that you could ring. The girls loved being free to run around outside and also loved to ring the bell. Was this stop the best place to take our young girls? In hindsight, no. But, looking back, it is a funny memory that we have.

When we have long trips to the doctor's office, we like to add fun activities to the itinerary for our girls. One of our favorite activities is visiting the Crayola Experience, where the girls can play, create, and enjoy age-appropriate activities. When we don't have time to visit a fun children's place, we let the girls choose the restaurants they want to eat at and use the hotel pool for swimming. I am constantly reminded that kids enjoy simple things and don't need extravagance.

During our trip to Arizona, we had several doctors' appointments over several days. In between appointments, we went swimming, visited a farm, a train depot, the zoo, and more. Doing fun activities as a family helped us enjoy our time together and is still a favorite memory many years later.

Our family memories are not always centered around doctors' visits. For example, one year we bought a season pass to SeaWorld and Aquatica. When we needed a weekend getaway, we enjoyed playing in the water and watching the shows there. We also did simpler things but made sure to do it as a family, such as arts and crafts, challenges, and day trips to play at the ocean. No matter the activity, we prioritize spending time together.

It's also important to find ways to remember these memories. Our family enjoys going through photo books, which the girls sometimes choose as bedtime stories. Other times, they just want to look back at their photo book with their baby pictures. Reviewing and discussing these memories brings us joy, especially during difficult times.

Furthermore, we collect small souvenirs from the places we visit and display them on a shelf. These souvenirs, such as cups, keychains, magnets, and even musical instruments, help us look back and remember our experiences. The girls still enjoy playing with the interactive items (drum, maraca, train whistle, etc.) we've collected.

A new favorite way to preserve memories and celebrate our girls and their journeys is through the Tiny Superheroes program. This fantastic program provides capes to kids with medical challenges, and you can then add patches to the cape to represent the different medical obstacles your child has overcome. Additionally, the program offers monthly challenges, providing another great opportunity to create lasting memories with your family.

No matter how big or small, these memories are something you can cherish for a lifetime. I encourage you to create as many positive memories as possible with your family!

**Helpful Programs/Ideas to Look Into:**

\* **Doctor Bag**: How many times have you been to the doctor's office, and your kiddo wants to watch a show on your phone, gets hungry and throws a fit, or is tired of sitting in the same small room for such a long time that they start going crazy? We went through too many of these experiences before I decided to make a bag that we only use and take with us to doctors' appointments. I included coloring books and supplies, tangrams, magnetic games, trivia cards, and more. Tailor the activities in this bag to your kiddos' interests, but only use it at doctors' appointments so they don't become bored. Consider switching out the items every so often.

\* **TinySuperheroes**: a way to honor, celebrate, and remember your child's health journey with a cape you get to customize for your kiddo. Check out this amazing program at their website:

https://tinysuperheroes.com/

\* The **Adventure Challenge**: books with fun activities for your family to do together. It can be easy to get stuck doing the same thing over and over again, but the Adventure Challenge Books allow you to make memories together that are spontaneous and different from your normal routine. The books also serve as a scrapbook of your memories. Check out The Adventure Challenge books at this link:

https://www.theadventurechallenge.com/

**\* Local Museums, Zoos, Splashpads, etc.**

**\*Car Scavenger Hunt:** for long road trips to doctors' appointments. Search for a car scavenger hunt online to find the option that looks best for your family.

**\* The Road Trip Game**: another game for long car rides. Look for this online at Walmart.

**\* Social Worker**: Ask a doctor to connect you with one. See what support they can offer. They have financial aid knowledge, program knowledge, and more!

**\* The Conqueror Virtual Challenges**: If you are struggling to stay active, these are fun challenges to encourage you to stay consistent. You get to pick virtual race paths and log the miles doing any activity you choose. They have fictional and real trails. Below is the link to check out this amazing site!

https://www.theconqueror.events

# Part 3

# An Affirmation

# Journey for

# Caregivers

In part three, there are 50 affirmations. Each affirmation has five different supporting activities to help you internalize the affirmation. There is a journaling space underneath each task so you can keep track of your journey and look back on the things you've learned. You can complete the journey in the order listed or mix-and-match based on your needs.

# Affirmations

1. I am not alone.
2. I am loved.
3. I am strong.
4. I am important.
5. I can feel peace.
6. I am an advocate for my child.
7. I am enough.
8. I am organized.
9. I live in the present.
10. Past experiences have made me stronger.
11. I can conquer anything.
12. I can smile and laugh.
13. I can plan ahead and prepare.
14. I can remember what is most important.
15. I can rest.
16. I can make good decisions for my child.
17. I am not weighed down by guilt or shame.
18. I can find calm in the waiting.
19. I am flexible.
20. I can stay active.

21. My experiences can help others.

22. I am grateful.

23. I create positive memories.

24. I am empathetic.

25. I can see the beauty in nature.

26. I accept and love my life.

27. Blame does not hold me back.

28. It is ok for me to feel all varieties of emotions.

29. My child has many strengths and gifts.

30. I create joy.

31. I continue to learn new things.

32. Some people won't understand my situation, and that's ok.

33. My life is unique.

34. I have needs, and they matter.

35. I speak up.

36. I find a good team of doctors and professionals.

37. I am talented.

38. I have hope.

39. I use available resources.

40. I am vulnerable.

41. I am firm like a rock.

42. I can find gifts (good things) in each day.

43. I know when to slow down and/or ask for assistance.

44. My world is colorful.

**45.** I live in a medically advanced time period.

**46.** I prioritize mental health.

**47.** I can make any environment feel like home.

**48.** I can find comfort.

**49.** I love being a parent.

**50.** I can zoom out and see the big picture.

**51.** Create your own affirmation and activities to accompany it.

# Affirmation 1

# I am not alone.

Medical tests and procedures make me feel isolated. Instead of doing play groups and socializing, I'm at therapy and specialist appointments. By the time I get home, I'm too tired to add one more thing to my day. My husband is usually at work, so I often attend my kiddos' appointments and surgeries alone. But no matter how alone you feel, you are not alone! This week, take the opportunity to identify your support group.

# Day 1

Make a list of anyone who provides you with assistance today, such as doctors, nurses, receptionists, or even the checkers at the grocery store.

_____

_____

_____

_____

_____

_____

_____

_____

_____

_____

_____

_____

_____

_____

_____

_____

_____

# **Day 2**

Make a list of your support group. This can include family, friends, therapists, or anyone else you can reach out to for help.

_____

_____

_____

_____

_____

_____

_____

_____

_____

_____

_____

_____

_____

_____

_____

_____

_____

_____

_____

_____

# Day 3

Write about an encounter with someone who showed they cared about you or your kiddo today.

_____

_____

_____

_____

_____

_____

_____

_____

_____

_____

_____

_____

_____

_____

_____

_____

# Day 4

Refer back to your list from Tuesday and choose one person to reach out to the next time you feel alone. Share your worries, what makes you happy, and any other challenges you are going through.

_____

_____

_____

_____

_____

_____

_____

_____

_____

_____

_____

_____

_____

_____

_____

_____

_____

_____

# Day 5

Think about all the doctors and specialists who help treat your kiddo. How are they a part of your support team?

_____

_____

_____

_____

_____

_____

_____

_____

_____

_____

_____

_____

_____

_____

_____

_____

_____

_____

_____

# Affirmation 2

# I am loved.

Feeling loved can keep you going even when you're tank is empty. There is something magical about knowing there are people who love you for you. Forgetting that you are loved comes all too naturally with exhaustion. This week, remember you are loved!

# Day 1

Make a list of people who love you. On the bad days, pull out the list to remind yourself other people care.

_____

_____

_____

_____

_____

_____

_____

_____

_____

_____

_____

_____

_____

_____

_____

_____

_____

_____

_____

# Day 2

How do your family members show you love? How do these expressions of love make you feel?

_____

_____

_____

_____

_____

_____

_____

_____

_____

_____

_____

_____

_____

_____

_____

_____

_____

_____

# Day 3

Look up multiple definitions of the word "love." Combine your favorite definitions or come up with your own. How can you hold on to the feeling of being loved when you are struggling?

_____

_____

_____

_____

_____

_____

_____

_____

_____

_____

_____

_____

_____

_____

_____

_____

# Day 4

Do you feel loved right now? Why or why not? If needed, spend some time problem solving.

_____

_____

_____

_____

_____

_____

_____

_____

_____

_____

_____

_____

_____

_____

_____

_____

_____

_____

# Day 5

Ponder about why you are worthy of love. Record your thoughts.

_____

_____

_____

_____

_____

_____

_____

_____

_____

_____

_____

_____

_____

_____

_____

_____

_____

_____

# Affirmation 3

# I am strong.

Self-doubt and discouragement are not hard to come across in the caregiving journey. You may not have time to do extravagant activities due to your kiddo's health. Your house may be messier than you'd like, or you may not be able to jump out of bed in the morning like other people you know. Despite these differences from what appears to be the norm, you are strong and have strengths.

# Day 1

What is something or someone that symbolizes strength? Why does this person or thing make you think of strength?

_____

_____

_____

_____

_____

_____

_____

_____

_____

_____

_____

_____

_____

_____

_____

_____

_____

_____

_____

_____

# Day 2

Think about a challenging situation(s) you conquered. How did you show strength during this time? (The answer could be as simple as getting out of bed each morning.)

_____

_____

_____

_____

_____

_____

_____

_____

_____

_____

_____

_____

_____

_____

_____

_____

_____

# Day 3

Make a list of hard things you have experienced. Title this list "Accomplishing/Experiencing Hard Things Resume." How did these experiences make you stronger?

_____

_____

_____

_____

_____

_____

_____

_____

_____

_____

_____

_____

_____

_____

_____

_____

_____

_____

# **Day 4**

Write about a time you felt strong. How can you recreate those feelings in yourself today?

---

# Day 5

Strength isn't about never getting discouraged or tired. Strength means that you persevere! Being a caregiver requires a lot of strength. Every time you start feeling discouraged today, remind yourself that you do hard things daily! How does this reminder affect your day?

_____

_____

_____

_____

_____

_____

_____

_____

_____

_____

_____

_____

_____

_____

_____

_____

_____

# Affirmation 4

# I am important.

Having a kiddo with many medical needs can keep you very busy. When you're preoccupied, you can forget about yourself and your value. When you forget to take care of yourself, everything seems harder! You also have needs and are important! Don't forget to make it a priority to take care of yourself too!

# Day 1

What can you do for yourself today? (eat at a restaurant, enjoy your favorite candy, get a milkshake, etc.) Make whatever you choose a priority for today.

_____

_____

_____

_____

_____

_____

_____

_____

_____

_____

_____

_____

_____

_____

_____

_____

_____

# Day 2

Who are you? Part of being important is knowing your identity. Caregiving can cause us to forget ourselves. Write a list of ten likes and dislikes.

_____

_____

_____

_____

_____

_____

_____

_____

_____

_____

_____

_____

_____

_____

_____

_____

_____

# Day 3

Search for self-care ideas online. Pick a suggestion and do it today.

_____

_____

_____

_____

_____

_____

_____

_____

_____

_____

_____

_____

_____

_____

_____

_____

_____

_____

_____

# Day 4

Running around to appointments, etc., can make it hard to eat healthy, balanced meals. Make sure you have at least one healthy, balanced meal today.

_____

_____

_____

_____

_____

_____

_____

_____

_____

_____

_____

_____

_____

_____

_____

_____

_____

_____

# Day 5

Research "love languages," a term from the book *The Five Love Languages* by Gary Chapman, and if you have time, take the quiz. How can knowing your "love language" help you move forward?

You can find information and the quiz at https://5lovelanguages.com.

_____

_____

_____

_____

_____

_____

_____

_____

_____

_____

_____

_____

_____

_____

_____

_____

_____

# Affirmation 5

# I can feel peace.

Amidst the chaos of caregiving, you can lose your sense of peace. This can leave you feeling drained, anxious, and discouraged. Below are some exercises to empower you to take charge and make your own peace. The way you find peace will be individual to you.

# **Day 1**

Go for a walk outside regardless of distance. Identify five beautiful things (it could be a sound, something you see, etc.) Even though you are living in a crazy moment, there is beauty to be found. Looking for and acknowledging this beauty can help you feel peace.

_____

_____

_____

_____

_____

_____

_____

_____

_____

_____

_____

_____

_____

_____

_____

# Day 2

Take 10 minutes (at least) for yourself today. Read a book, listen to music, close your eyes, or do something else you choose: no phone, no demands, just you in a place of your choosing. Write a few sentences about how you feel afterward.

_____

_____

_____

_____

_____

_____

_____

_____

_____

_____

_____

_____

_____

_____

_____

_____

# Day 3

What helps you feel relaxed? Some people color, some people write, some people go on a walk, some people sit outside, and much more. Try a new way to relax and feel peace today.

# Day 4

Often, things in our environment can take away our feelings of peace. Note one thing that is not peaceful in your current environment that you can control. (sink full of dishes, laundry basket overflowing, etc.) Create more peace today by getting rid of a small amount of discord.

_____

_____

_____

_____

_____

_____

_____

_____

_____

_____

_____

_____

_____

_____

_____

_____

# **Day 5**

Look back at the activities from Monday through Thursday. Acknowledge what helped you feel most peaceful. Repeat that activity again.

_____

_____

_____

_____

_____

_____

_____

_____

_____

_____

_____

_____

_____

_____

_____

_____

_____

_____

# Affirmation 6

# I am an advocate for my child.

Advocates play a crucial role in various aspects of life. Examples of advocates include attorneys, teachers, and parents. Advocates stand up for and support those who can't fully advocate for themselves. For example, having a discussion in the legal world is like speaking a whole different language. Legal jargon is not common knowledge. So, attorneys use their knowledge of legal terminology and laws to represent and defend their clients. Teachers advocate for their students by monitoring their progress and addressing any necessary actions to ensure the best for each student. Many times, children don't understand what is happening with their bodies or know how to communicate their feelings and more. Parents advocate for their kids by learning everything they can about their kids and using their more advanced vocabulary and life experiences to speak up to doctors and other professionals.

# Day 1

Look up the definition and synonyms for the word "advocate."
How do you advocate for your child?

_____

_____

_____

_____

_____

_____

_____

_____

_____

_____

_____

_____

_____

_____

_____

_____

_____

_____

_____

_____

# __Day 2__

It's easy to forget the questions and thoughts you have for doctors and therapists. Write down two or more of your most pressing questions for your next appointment.

_____

_____

_____

_____

_____

_____

_____

_____

_____

_____

_____

_____

_____

_____

_____

_____

_____

_____

# **Day 3**

You know your child better than anyone else. What are your kiddo's strengths and weaknesses? How are you helping your kiddo overcome weaknesses and maintain or improve strengths?

_____

_____

_____

_____

_____

_____

_____

_____

_____

_____

_____

_____

_____

_____

_____

_____

_____

_____

# Day 4

Review your recent visit notes and/or request a copy of your kiddo's records. Records are valuable tools for advocators.

_____

_____

_____

_____

_____

_____

_____

_____

_____

_____

_____

_____

_____

_____

_____

_____

_____

_____

# Day 5

To be an advocate, you need to understand who you're advocating for. Have a genuine conversation today, focused on your kiddo's feelings, hopes, and dreams. If your kiddo is too young, keep a medical journal to track their symptoms.

_____

_____

_____

_____

_____

_____

_____

_____

_____

_____

_____

_____

_____

_____

_____

_____

_____

# Affirmation 7

# I am enough.

It's common to feel inadequate as a caregiver. Most caregivers don't have previous medical training and learn on the job. Administering medical treatments that you previously assumed only happened at the doctors' offices can cause feelings of inferiority. But, regardless of your background, you are the person who loves your child the most. You are enough for this job!

# Day 1

Write a list of all the new skills/things you have learned in your time as a caregiver, and take a minute to celebrate your new knowledge.

_____

_____

_____

_____

_____

_____

_____

_____

_____

_____

_____

_____

_____

_____

_____

_____

_____

_____

_____

# Day 2

Identify your strengths and explain how they help you be a better caregiver.

_____

_____

_____

_____

_____

_____

_____

_____

_____

_____

_____

_____

_____

_____

_____

_____

_____

_____

_____

# Day 3

Acknowledge your weaknesses and write down how being a caregiver is helping you overcome them.

_____

_____

_____

_____

_____

_____

_____

_____

_____

_____

_____

_____

_____

_____

_____

_____

_____

_____

# Day 4

Reflect on who you are and how knowing yourself helps you realize that you are enough for the caregiver position.

_____

_____

_____

_____

_____

_____

_____

_____

_____

_____

_____

_____

_____

_____

_____

_____

_____

# Day 5

Consider previous life experiences that have prepared you for caregiving and explain how these experiences uniquely qualify you for the job.

_____

_____

_____

_____

_____

_____

_____

_____

_____

_____

_____

_____

_____

_____

_____

_____

_____

# Affirmation 8

# I am organized.

Being organized is an essential skill of a caregiver. It allows us to know the when, where, why, and how. Getting organized can be overwhelming, but once you get there, the benefits are well worth it!

# Day 1

What tool helps you stay the most organized (planner, phone, journal, timers, apps, etc.), and how has this tool made your life as a caregiver easier?

_____

_____

_____

_____

_____

_____

_____

_____

_____

_____

_____

_____

_____

_____

_____

_____

_____

# Day 2

Research different organizational tools and strategies. Choose a new organizational method to try for a day, such as a meal plan or a timer app.

_____

_____

_____

_____

_____

_____

_____

_____

_____

_____

_____

_____

_____

_____

_____

_____

_____

_____

# Day 3

How can you prioritize self-care in your busy schedule? Make it a priority for at least 5-10 minutes each day.

_____

_____

_____

_____

_____

_____

_____

_____

_____

_____

_____

_____

_____

_____

_____

_____

_____

_____

# Day 4

What is something that will make your life and being organized easier, such as a new cookbook, whiteboard calendar, or journal? Find what you think would help and purchase it or start saving for it.

_____

_____

_____

_____

_____

_____

_____

_____

_____

_____

_____

_____

_____

_____

_____

_____

_____

# Day 5

How do you organize your kiddo's records? Do you use a binder, file folders, filing cabinet, or something else? Research ways to organize medical records and choose the method that works best for you.

_____

_____

_____

_____

_____

_____

_____

_____

_____

_____

_____

_____

_____

_____

_____

_____

_____

_____

# Affirmation 9

# I live in the

# present.

As a caregiver, we often worry and stress about future tests, treatments, surgeries, and more. Worrying about the future causes an increase in anxiety. Alternatively, you might beat yourself up over a decision you wish you could have made differently in the past. This week, we will focus on being present to reduce anxiety.

# Day 1

Choose one family member. What is their favorite thing to do with you? Put all distractions aside and be 100% present for ten minutes with this family member doing one of their favorite things.

_____

_____

_____

_____

_____

_____

_____

_____

_____

_____

_____

_____

_____

_____

_____

_____

# Day 2

Sit alone without distractions for five minutes. Write down a list of all the information your senses provide: things you taste, smell, hear, feel, and see.

_____

_____

_____

_____

_____

_____

_____

_____

_____

_____

_____

_____

_____

_____

_____

_____

_____

# Day 3

Write a list of things you are grateful for today. The smaller the thing, the better! ☺

_____

_____

_____

_____

_____

_____

_____

_____

_____

_____

_____

_____

_____

_____

_____

_____

_____

_____

_____

# Day 4

Take a moment to write a letter to someone or a journal entry.

_____

_____

_____

_____

_____

_____

_____

_____

_____

_____

_____

_____

_____

_____

_____

_____

_____

_____

_____

# Day 5

Try living today in sections. Only look ahead in small periods of time. Once that time finishes, then look ahead a little bit more. How does this help you feel during the course of the day?

_____

_____

_____

_____

_____

_____

_____

_____

_____

_____

_____

_____

_____

_____

_____

_____

_____

# Affirmation 10

# Past experiences have made me stronger.

Difficult experiences can often weigh us down and add to the stress in our lives. Instead of becoming weighed down with one more thing, you can use past experiences to your benefit. You can learn from them and move forward.

# Day 1

Think about an experience you had as a young kid that was hard but helped you grow as a person.

_____

_____

_____

_____

_____

_____

_____

_____

_____

_____

_____

_____

_____

_____

_____

_____

_____

_____

# Day 2

Recall a difficult experience you had as a teenager. What tools did you use to overcome this challenge?

_____

_____

_____

_____

_____

_____

_____

_____

_____

_____

_____

_____

_____

_____

_____

_____

_____

_____

# Day 3

Reflect on an experience you had as an adult that wasn't easy. What tools did you use to overcome this challenge?

_____

_____

_____

_____

_____

_____

_____

_____

_____

_____

_____

_____

_____

_____

_____

_____

_____

_____

_____

_____

# Day 4

Look back at these experiences. What life lessons did you learn? How are they helping you today?

_____

_____

_____

_____

_____

_____

_____

_____

_____

_____

_____

_____

_____

_____

_____

_____

_____

_____

# Day 5

Identify some of your strongest personality traits. How do these traits help you as a caregiver?

_____

_____

_____

_____

_____

_____

_____

_____

_____

_____

_____

_____

_____

_____

_____

_____

_____

_____

# Affirmation 11

# I can conquer anything.

Today, remind yourself that you are capable of conquering anything that comes your way. Determination and perseverance can help you overcome any challenge. Tell yourself that you believe in your strength and ability to succeed.

# Day 1

Make a list of things you need to do but have been putting off. Choose one task and make sure to work on or complete it today. How did conquering this task make you feel?

_____

_____

_____

_____

_____

_____

_____

_____

_____

_____

_____

_____

_____

_____

_____

_____

_____

_____

_____

# **Day 2**

Medical decisions and diagnoses often come with many unknowns. What is the most concerning unknown for you right now? How can you increase your knowledge or learn about this issue to conquer the unknown?

_____

_____

_____

_____

_____

_____

_____

_____

_____

_____

_____

_____

_____

_____

_____

_____

# Day 3

Make a list of current medical issues that are within and outside of your control. Remind yourself that you can't control everything, and try to conquer any anxiety related to issues out of your control.

_____

_____

_____

_____

_____

_____

_____

_____

_____

_____

_____

_____

_____

_____

_____

_____

_____

_____

_____

# Day 4

What is one self-care activity you can do today? As a caregiver, it's easy to forget about your own needs. Conquer this issue today by doing something to take care of yourself.

_____

_____

_____

_____

_____

_____

_____

_____

_____

_____

_____

_____

_____

_____

_____

_____

_____

# Day 5

Find something new that you want to conquer, whether it's a new exercise program, cooking a new recipe, or reading a book. Work on conquering this new thing.

_____

_____

_____

_____

_____

_____

_____

_____

_____

_____

_____

_____

_____

_____

_____

_____

_____

_____

# Affirmation 12

# I can smile and laugh.

Being a caregiver can leave you breathless and eventually make you feel like you're just going through the motions of life. This week, let's focus on creating purposeful happiness.

# Day 1

Try to smile at everyone you interact with today. It could be just what they need, and it can also boost your own mood!

_____

_____

_____

_____

_____

_____

_____

_____

_____

_____

_____

_____

_____

_____

_____

_____

_____

_____

_____

# Day 2

Find something that makes you laugh, such as a movie, book, or joke. Share this humor with someone else.

_____

_____

_____

_____

_____

_____

_____

_____

_____

_____

_____

_____

_____

_____

_____

_____

_____

_____

# Day 3

Find something that makes your kiddo laugh and see how contagious their happiness is to you.

_____

_____

_____

_____

_____

_____

_____

_____

_____

_____

_____

_____

_____

_____

_____

_____

_____

# Day 4

Spend a few minutes with one of your favorite things, whether it's candy, a scented candle, or exercise. After, take a moment to smile.

_____

_____

_____

_____

_____

_____

_____

_____

_____

_____

_____

_____

_____

_____

_____

_____

_____

# Day 5

Look back at some of your favorite family memories. You can look through photos, watch old family videos, or look at photo books. What is your favorite memory that you saw during this experience? How many times did you smile?

_____

_____

_____

_____

_____

_____

_____

_____

_____

_____

_____

_____

_____

_____

_____

_____

_____

# Affirmation 13

# I can plan ahead and prepare.

Preparation is key to so many things in life. We prepare for travel, moving, cooking, sports, performances, and more. Preparation allows things to go much smoother. Caregiving is another important part of life that requires preparation.

# Day 1

Many times, medical issues arise that are urgent and unexpected. What is something you can do to plan ahead for the next time one of the unexpected incidents occurs? (Examples: prepare a freezer meal, ask a friend for help with childcare, etc.)

_____

_____

_____

_____

_____

_____

_____

_____

_____

_____

_____

_____

_____

_____

# Day 2

Recall a time in your life that you planned ahead and saw numerous benefits as a result. What benefits did you experience?

_____

_____

_____

_____

_____

_____

_____

_____

_____

_____

_____

_____

_____

_____

_____

_____

_____

# **Day 3**

Think about a time that you wish you had been more prepared for an event. What feelings did you express? For the future, how will you make sure you're more prepared?

_____

_____

_____

_____

_____

_____

_____

_____

_____

_____

_____

_____

_____

_____

_____

_____

_____

_____

# Day 4

Sometimes, there is just not time to prepare before, something suddenly happens and we have to act in response. How can you mentally prepare for handling the unknown? What positive thing can you tell yourself in a similar situation?

_____

_____

_____

_____

_____

_____

_____

_____

_____

_____

_____

_____

_____

_____

_____

_____

_____

# Day 5

Think about the steps of preparing a meal. Cooking requires analyzing the recipe, making a list, getting the ingredients from the store, preparing any ingredients, following the recipe, and then cleaning-up at the end. Caregiving is similar; some things we can complete in advance, like making a grocery list and shopping, while other things have to be done right before cooking the food, such as combining the ingredients. What are some short-term and long-term things you can prepare to make your caregiving journey easier?

_____

_____

_____

_____

_____

_____

_____

_____

_____

_____

_____

_____

_____

_____

# Affirmation 14

# I can remember what is most important.

Many times, as caregivers, you run from one thing to the next, to the next. It can make your day pretty mindless, and we can even forget that everything we're doing is for our loved ones. This week, we will focus on making sure to remember the real reason we do what we do.

# Day 1

Choose a special activity to do with your loved one. Whether it's playing, coloring, or going to the park, spend at least 10 minutes of focused, intentional, one-on-one time with them. Try to avoid looking at your phone during this time.

_____

_____

_____

_____

_____

_____

_____

_____

_____

_____

_____

_____

_____

_____

_____

_____

# Day 2

Plan a family activity, such as going to the beach, having a family dinner, or a movie night. Be present and pay attention to how often your loved one laughs. Take some notes about what, if anything, is bothering them.

_____

_____

_____

_____

_____

_____

_____

_____

_____

_____

_____

_____

_____

_____

_____

_____

_____

_____

# Day 3

Take some time to take care of yourself. Remember the pre-flight safety instructions about putting on your oxygen mask before helping anyone else. Today, do something to take care of yourself to ensure you have what it takes to be a great caregiver.

_____

_____

_____

_____

_____

_____

_____

_____

_____

_____

_____

_____

_____

_____

_____

_____

_____

_____

# Day 4

How can you show your significant other that you love and care about them? Do something for them today to express these feelings.

_____

_____

_____

_____

_____

_____

_____

_____

_____

_____

_____

_____

_____

_____

_____

_____

_____

# Day 5

How can you express love to your child today? Do something for them today to express these feelings.

_____

_____

_____

_____

_____

_____

_____

_____

_____

_____

_____

_____

_____

_____

_____

_____

_____

_____

_____

# **Affirmation 15**

# I can rest.

Balancing all the medical tasks can make the day fly by, leaving a long list of unfinished tasks. After the kids go to bed, it's tempting to rush to catch up. This week, prioritize rest.

# Day 1

After the kids go to bed, set aside the to-do list, relax on the couch or in bed, and watch a show or a movie. Take note of how you feel the next morning.

_____

_____

_____

_____

_____

_____

_____

_____

_____

_____

_____

_____

_____

_____

_____

_____

_____

# Day 2

Make every effort to get 8 hours of sleep tonight. How does getting this amount of sleep impact your day?

_____

_____

_____

_____

_____

_____

_____

_____

_____

_____

_____

_____

_____

_____

_____

_____

_____

_____

# Day 3

Arrange for a babysitter or ask your significant other or a friend to watch the kids. Take some time to do something relaxing (have dinner at a restaurant with no cooking or clean up, watch a movie, grab coffee with a friend, etc.) How did you feel after completing your relaxing activity?

_____

_____

_____

_____

_____

_____

_____

_____

_____

_____

_____

_____

_____

_____

_____

_____

# Day 4

Allow your kids to watch a show or have screen time for 15-30 minutes. Use this time to rest, nap, watch a show, or do whatever you need in that moment. Did this break help you feel recharged?

_____

_____

_____

_____

_____

_____

_____

_____

_____

_____

_____

_____

_____

_____

_____

_____

_____

# Day 5

Do your best to get another night of 8 hours of sleep. Try to make this a regular habit. How do you feel when you have gotten multiple nights of 8 hours of sleep in a row?

_____

_____

_____

_____

_____

_____

_____

_____

_____

_____

_____

_____

_____

_____

_____

_____

_____

_____

# Affirmation 16

# I can make good decisions for my child.

It is normal to be bombarded with lots of information and opinions about what the best treatment options are for your kids, especially ones struggling with medical diagnoses. This week, we will focus on weeding out the background noise and using accurate information to make the best decisions for the people you care about.

# Day 1

In high school, there was always a list of sources that our teachers wouldn't let us use when citing research in a paper. These sites were known not to be accurate, and our teachers didn't want us to use incorrect information. Find 2-3 reputable sources that talk about your child's medical condition. (Often, these websites end in .gov, .edu, etc., and or are written by actual doctors at actual medical facilities). Look into different treatment options and trust your parental instincts to make a decision. What did your research teach you, and what decision did you make?

_____

_____

_____

_____

_____

_____

_____

_____

_____

_____

_____

_____

_____

# Day 2

Seek opinions from various specialists to form a well-rounded care plan for your child. If a treatment plan doesn't sit right with you, seek another specialist for a second opinion.

_____

_____

_____

_____

_____

_____

_____

_____

_____

_____

_____

_____

_____

_____

_____

_____

_____

_____

# Day 3

Take a minute to reflect on your feelings towards your child. Jot these feelings down. Most likely, love was a feeling that you recorded. Always make your decisions out of love. What future decisions will you make out of love, and how does knowing that decisions are made with love make you feel better about any uncertainty?

_____

_____

_____

_____

_____

_____

_____

_____

_____

_____

_____

_____

_____

_____

_____

# **Day 4**

Recall a previous positive medical decision you made and its successful outcome. Use this experience to strengthen your confidence and ability to make the next decision.

_____

_____

_____

_____

_____

_____

_____

_____

_____

_____

_____

_____

_____

_____

_____

_____

_____

_____

# Day 5

Write down an upcoming decision you have to make for your child. Make a list of pros and cons for both options and use this list to help make your decision. Did this strategy make it easier to make a choice? Will you use this strategy to help you make future decisions?

_____

_____

_____

_____

_____

_____

_____

_____

_____

_____

_____

_____

_____

_____

_____

_____

_____

# Affirmation 17

# I am not weighed down by guilt or shame.

It is natural to second guess, feel guilty, or wonder about the outcomes of different choices. However, dwelling on the past won't change it. Instead, focus on making positive decisions in the present. Feelings of guilt and shame can hold you back, instill fear, and hinder your ability to live in the present.

# **Day 1**

Reflect on something for which you currently feel guilty or shameful about in your role as a caretaker. Consider whether this decision or action was within your control. If it was, think about how you can use what you learned from it to help you today and down the road.

_____

_____

_____

_____

_____

_____

_____

_____

_____

_____

_____

_____

_____

_____

_____

_____

_____

# **Day 2**

Create a list of things that are within and outside of your control. Identify any items on your list for which you feel guilty but have no control over. Remind yourself that these things were beyond your control. For those that were within your control, consider how you can make different choices moving forward, while reminding yourself you are constantly learning and improving.

_____

_____

_____

_____

_____

_____

_____

_____

_____

_____

_____

_____

_____

_____

_____

_____

# Day 3

Take a minute to list everything you have learned through your caretaking experience. Acknowledge and celebrate the knowledge and skills you've gained. While you may not have pursued formal education in caretaking, circumstances led you to learn and grow. Remember, knowledge is power.

_____

_____

_____

_____

_____

_____

_____

_____

_____

_____

_____

_____

_____

_____

_____

_____

_____

# Day 4

Look up the definitions of "guilt" and "shame." Reflect on how your caregiver journey can trigger these emotions. Consider how feelings of guilt and shame affect you. Acknowledge how these emotions restrict you from being your best self. When these feelings arise, push them away and remind yourself of their detrimental impact on you and your family.

_____

_____

_____

_____

_____

_____

_____

_____

_____

_____

_____

_____

_____

_____

_____

# Day 5

Consider how you interact with others when feeling guilty or ashamed. Evaluate whether this aligns with how you want to treat people. Strive to be more mindful of feelings of guilt or shame and choose to respond in a positive manner rather than defaulting to your natural inclinations.

# Affirmation 18

# I can find calm in

# the waiting.

The role of a caregiver often involves a lot of waiting, whether it's waiting for a doctor's call, waiting for a procedure, waiting for test results, or waiting to see if treatment is effective. It's important to find ways to relax during these waiting periods, as being unable to do so can negatively impact your physical health and prevent you from fully enjoying life.

# Day 1

Spend some one-on-one time with your kiddo. Be fully present and minimize distractions. Notice how this affects your sense of calm.

_____

_____

_____

_____

_____

_____

_____

_____

_____

_____

_____

_____

_____

_____

_____

_____

_____

_____

# Day 2

Monitor your anxiety levels today. When you feel anxious, take a few minutes to close your eyes, take deep breaths, and listen to the sounds around you.

_____

_____

_____

_____

_____

_____

_____

_____

_____

_____

_____

_____

_____

_____

_____

_____

_____

# Day 3

Research different relaxation and mindfulness techniques. Choose one to try today and take note of how it makes you feel.

_____

_____

_____

_____

_____

_____

_____

_____

_____

_____

_____

_____

_____

_____

_____

_____

_____

_____

_____

# **Day 4**

Find at least five minutes to just sit and relax without any distractions. Focus on your breathing. How does focusing on this one thing impact you?

_____

_____

_____

_____

_____

_____

_____

_____

_____

_____

_____

_____

_____

_____

_____

_____

_____

# Day 5

Identify something you can do today that you won't be able to do when the waiting period is over. Make it a priority to do that activity today.

_____

_____

_____

_____

_____

_____

_____

_____

_____

_____

_____

_____

_____

_____

_____

_____

_____

_____

# Affirmation 19

# I am flexible.

If you've been a caregiver long enough, you're aware that plans can suddenly change. Appointments may need to be rescheduled, surgery dates can shift, and medication shortages can occur. Feeling anxious or negative about these uncontrollable events can consume your time and energy. Being flexible, however, allows you to adapt to changes and make the most of your time without getting stuck in what you can't control.

# Day 1

Think of a time when something unexpected happened medically. How did you handle it?

_____

_____

_____

_____

_____

_____

_____

_____

_____

_____

_____

_____

_____

_____

_____

_____

_____

_____

_____

_____

# Day 2

What is something you can remove from your to-do list today to make time for something more urgent?

_____

_____

_____

_____

_____

_____

_____

_____

_____

_____

_____

_____

_____

_____

_____

_____

_____

_____

_____

# **Day 3**

Recall a time when your original plans changed. How did the new outcome possibly work better than the original plan?

_____

_____

_____

_____

_____

_____

_____

_____

_____

_____

_____

_____

_____

_____

_____

_____

_____

_____

_____

_____

# Day 4

Look back to a time when waiting longer had unforeseen benefits. What were the benefits?

_____

_____

_____

_____

_____

_____

_____

_____

_____

_____

_____

_____

_____

_____

_____

_____

_____

_____

# Day 5

Write yourself a note to read the next time plans change. What wisdom have you gained this week that will help your future self? Remember to be kind! ☺

_____

_____

_____

_____

_____

_____

_____

_____

_____

_____

_____

_____

_____

_____

_____

_____

_____

_____

# Affirmation 20

# I can stay active.

There is a wealth of medical research showing that staying active can keep you healthier. Often, when you are taking care of someone else, their to-do list takes priority, and your own needs quickly drop to the bottom of the list. By taking care of yourself first, you ensure that you have the health, strength, and energy to take care of others.

# Day 1

Take a walk that lasts at least 10 minutes. If possible, go outside and take notice of all the small details nature has to offer (such as types of trees, flowers, cloud shapes, etc.). If you can't go outside, try to observe things indoors that you don't normally pay attention to. How do you feel after walking for ten minutes?

_____

_____

_____

_____

_____

_____

_____

_____

_____

_____

_____

_____

_____

_____

_____

_____

# **Day 2**

YouTube is an amazing tool that can be very helpful, especially for caregivers. It's almost impossible to find time to go to a gym or take athletic classes when you are caring for someone else, but YouTube has some amazing resources that can save you time. Search for a 5-10 minute workout of your choice. If you want something relaxing, try yoga; if you want something intense, look for something under the cardio or HIIT categories. How do you feel after completing this activity? Is it an exercise you will try again, or will you avoid this type in the future?

_____

_____

_____

_____

_____

_____

_____

_____

_____

_____

_____

# Day 3

When spending a lot of time in doctors' offices and hospitals, it's easy to find yourself and your kiddo sitting around all day. Today, find an activity that you and your kiddo can do together to get up and moving. It could be an obstacle course, walking laps around the hospital, playing at the park, etc. How did adding more activity to your day change how you felt at the end of the day?

_____

_____

_____

_____

_____

_____

_____

_____

_____

_____

_____

_____

_____

_____

_____

_____

# Day 4

Refer back to Tuesday's challenge. Try a different video or type of exercise. Record how you feel.

_____

_____

_____

_____

_____

_____

_____

_____

_____

_____

_____

_____

_____

_____

_____

_____

_____

_____

# Day 5

Many people find it challenging to stay active when doing it alone. Find someone to be active with today (a friend, spouse, etc.). How does it make you feel to be active with a support person? Was it too complicated to add something else to your schedule, or will you try to make this part of your routine?

_____

_____

_____

_____

_____

_____

_____

_____

_____

_____

_____

_____

_____

_____

_____

_____

_____

# Affirmation 21

# My experiences can help others.

When you're in the midst of caregiving, you might wish for someone who understands what you're going through, while feeling like no one does. However, because of your experiences, you can now be someone who understands and supports others in similar situations. You can use your knowledge to help others on their caregiving journey.

# Day 1

Think of someone in your family or friend circle who is facing challenges. Reach out to them by sending a text, flowers, a small gift, or any gesture to let them know that you see their struggles and that they are doing great. Show them your support and willingness to be there for them.

_____

_____

_____

_____

_____

_____

_____

_____

_____

_____

_____

_____

_____

_____

_____

# Day 2

Pay attention to the people around you and try to identify if they need help with something. Take small actions to support them, such as offering a listening ear, comforting a family member, or keeping someone company if they seem anxious. Make notes of your experience.

_____

_____

_____

_____

_____

_____

_____

_____

_____

_____

_____

_____

_____

_____

_____

_____

_____

# Day 3

Reflect on your time as a caregiver and think about the advice you would offer to someone else in a similar situation. Identify who could benefit from this advice and how you can share it with them.

_____

_____

_____

_____

_____

_____

_____

_____

_____

_____

_____

_____

_____

_____

_____

_____

_____

_____

# Day 4

Think back to your toughest days and determine what you wished someone would have done for you. Consider how you can fulfill that need for someone else going through a similar situation.

_____

_____

_____

_____

_____

_____

_____

_____

_____

_____

_____

_____

_____

_____

_____

_____

_____

_____

# Day 5

Consider how you can share the lessons you've learned from being a caregiver with others. Explore different options, such as joining support groups, participating in online communities, or starting a blog to share your experiences and insights. Choose one method to share what you've learned, and reflect on the impact it has. How did it feel to be able to help someone else in a similar situation?

_____

_____

_____

_____

_____

_____

_____

_____

_____

_____

_____

_____

_____

_____

# Affirmation 22

# I am grateful.

There are so many things in life to be grateful for, but it's easy to not recognize them when we're rushing around engaged in our caregiving responsibilities. The difficult aspects of caregiving can make it easy to forget to appreciate the good things in life. This week, we will focus on remembering to see what we are grateful for daily.

# Day 1

Make a list of at least 10 things you are grateful for. Reflect on how these things have positively impacted your life.

_____

_____

_____

_____

_____

_____

_____

_____

_____

_____

_____

_____

_____

_____

_____

_____

_____

_____

_____

_____

# Day 2

Think of someone who helped you during your caregiving journey. Reach out and express your gratitude. Be specific about how they supported you and why you are grateful for them.

_____

_____

_____

_____

_____

_____

_____

_____

_____

_____

_____

_____

_____

_____

_____

_____

_____

_____

# Day 3

Reflect on your caregiving experiences and list a few things you have learned. Contemplate how to show gratitude for this knowledge.

_____

_____

_____

_____

_____

_____

_____

_____

_____

_____

_____

_____

_____

_____

_____

_____

_____

# Day 4

Recall a time when something didn't go as planned. With hindsight, reflect on why you are grateful for how things turned out rather than how they were initially planned.

_____

_____

_____

_____

_____

_____

_____

_____

_____

_____

_____

_____

_____

_____

_____

_____

# Day 5

Write a note or a quick message to each member of your immediate family or friends. Share why you are grateful for them in your life. Reflect on how focusing on gratitude made you feel throughout the week, and consider how to incorporate gratitude into your everyday life.

_____

_____

_____

_____

_____

_____

_____

_____

_____

_____

_____

_____

_____

_____

_____

_____

# Affirmation 23

# I create positive memories.

One of my favorite memories as a kid was our summer vacations. My dad always told me that memories can last a lifetime. They are also something positive we can hold onto and remember during tough times, giving us hope for better days.

# Day 1

Make a list of some of your favorite past memories. Now, make a list of some memories you want to create (like a bucket list). How can you make these dreams, or at least one of them, a reality?

_____

_____

_____

_____

_____

_____

_____

_____

_____

_____

_____

_____

_____

_____

_____

_____

_____

_____

# Day 2

Plan to create a special memory today. It can be a memory of having a special dinner where everyone is dressed up, a fun pizza night, a movie night, etc. Do something special that you and your kids can remember and look back on. How do you feel after focusing on making a positive memory today?

_____

_____

_____

_____

_____

_____

_____

_____

_____

_____

_____

_____

_____

_____

_____

# Day 3

Memories have the power to allow us to look back and remember or even relive our favorite things that happened in the past. But, in order to do that, usually you have to do something to preserve that memory. Think about and choose a way to preserve something you want to remember. You could scrapbook, make an online photo book, create a small video, write in your journal, etc.

_____

_____

_____

_____

_____

_____

_____

_____

_____

_____

_____

_____

_____

_____

_____

# Day 4

List some simple memories. Try to make a small positive memory a part of your daily/weekly routine. This routine can look like a hug goodbye in the morning, a weekly ice cream date, a recurring movie night, a weekly phone call, etc. How does it make you feel to have something to look forward to each day/week?

_____

_____

_____

_____

_____

_____

_____

_____

_____

_____

_____

_____

_____

_____

_____

_____

# Day 5

Look back at old photos, videos, family journal entries, etc. How do you feel after reviewing positive memories from the past? Does remembering give you a different perspective on life?

_____

_____

_____

_____

_____

_____

_____

_____

_____

_____

_____

_____

_____

_____

_____

_____

_____

_____

_____

# Affirmation 24

# I am empathetic.

As a caregiver, I'm sure you can look back and remember a time when you received news you didn't want to hear, sat nervously in a waiting room, anxiously expected test results, and more uncomfortable scenarios. In those moments, you likely wanted someone to understand and empathize with you. Be the person you need for someone else in need.

# Day 1

Research the definition of "empathy." Think of someone in your life who embodies empathy. What specific actions can you take to incorporate their empathetic qualities into your own skill set?

_____

_____

_____

_____

_____

_____

_____

_____

_____

_____

_____

_____

_____

_____

_____

_____

_____

# Day 2

Reflect on a time when someone showed you empathy. How did their actions make you feel? What specific behaviors or gestures contributed to this feeling? How can you replicate this scenario for others?

_____

_____

_____

_____

_____

_____

_____

_____

_____

_____

_____

_____

_____

_____

_____

_____

# Day 3

Keep an eye out for anyone who might be struggling today. Reach out to them with empathy. Send a thoughtful text or make a quick phone call to show that you genuinely care.

_____

_____

_____

_____

_____

_____

_____

_____

_____

_____

_____

_____

_____

_____

_____

_____

_____

_____

# Day 4

One day, my daughter came home with a school award for demonstrating "purposeful empathy." I love that phrase! What, in your opinion, does it mean to show purposeful empathy? Why do you think it's important to be purposeful when empathizing with others?

_____

_____

_____

_____

_____

_____

_____

_____

_____

_____

_____

_____

_____

_____

_____

_____

# Day 5

Recall a past situation that lacked empathy. Rewrite the scenario to include empathy. How does infusing empathy into the situation change the outcome and your emotions related to it?

_____

_____

_____

_____

_____

_____

_____

_____

_____

_____

_____

_____

_____

_____

_____

_____

_____

_____

# Affirmation 25

# I can see the

# beauty in nature.

When juggling appointments and rushing from one place to another, it's easy to overlook the beauty that surrounds us. I often find myself forgetting to appreciate nature amidst all the caregiving responsibilities. There are countless wonderful things outdoors that we tend to miss when we're preoccupied. This week, take some time to focus on the nature around you.

# Day 1

Step outside and make a list of five things that you see every day but typically fail to notice. Write down a few details about each item on your list.

_____

_____

_____

_____

_____

_____

_____

_____

_____

_____

_____

_____

_____

_____

_____

_____

_____

# Day 2

What is your favorite natural scenery? Why do you love it? Find a picture of this scenery and imagine being there. What do you smell, taste, touch, feel, and hear?

_____

_____

_____

_____

_____

_____

_____

_____

_____

_____

_____

_____

_____

_____

_____

_____

_____

# Day 3

Nature includes the seasons of the year. Recognize the current season of the year where you live. Google some ways to celebrate the season. (Example in autumn, find leaves and make a print with crayons or paint. In winter, make a snowman or go skiing in the mountains. In spring, plant a flower or take pictures of flowers that are starting to grow. In summer, lay in the sun and look at the clouds or go to the beach or go on a hike.) How did celebrating the current season help you appreciate nature and what is right outside?

_____

_____

_____

_____

_____

_____

_____

_____

_____

_____

_____

_____

# Day 4

Choose a simple art project that celebrates your favorite aspect of nature. For instance, paint a nature-themed picture or collect and display seashells. Place this reminder somewhere you can see it daily as a way to encourage yourself to always appreciate the beauty outside, no matter what else is going on.

_____

_____

_____

_____

_____

_____

_____

_____

_____

_____

_____

_____

_____

_____

_____

# Day 5

Take a short nature walk and make a list of things you see, hear, feel, smell, and taste. Mark the one thing that stood out the most to you. Why did this particular thing capture your attention more than the rest?

_____

_____

_____

_____

_____

_____

_____

_____

_____

_____

_____

_____

_____

_____

_____

_____

_____

_____

# **Affirmation 26**

# I accept and love

# my life.

It's easy to compare ourselves to others and think that they are living the life of our dreams, but comparison can be so harmful to our families and us. However, as I've grown older, I've realized that everyone faces their own challenges, whether these are visible to the outside world or not. This means that nobody is living the perfect life we imagine they are. We often wish away our own difficulties, but constantly wishing for something else can make us very unhappy. This week, let's focus on being okay with our own challenges and work on loving life.

# Day 1

Reflect on your teenage dreams of your future family and compare them to your current life. How do your dreams differ from reality? Identify the positive aspects of your life today due to your role as a caregiver.

_____

_____

_____

_____

_____

_____

_____

_____

_____

_____

_____

_____

_____

_____

_____

_____

_____

# Day 2

Identify your favorite part of daily life and explain how it contributes to accepting and loving your current situation. What do you look forward to every day? How does this thing help you enjoy your life in the day-to-day moments?

_____

_____

_____

_____

_____

_____

_____

_____

_____

_____

_____

_____

_____

_____

_____

_____

# Day 3

Take some time to journal about your past caregiving experiences and express your feelings.

_____

_____

_____

_____

_____

_____

_____

_____

_____

_____

_____

_____

_____

_____

_____

_____

_____

_____

_____

# Day 4

Think of a small activity that can enhance your appreciation for your daily life. Create a list of a few activities that only take a few minutes each day. (Examples: Read a book for five minutes, eat a piece of chocolate, say a private prayer, journal, etc.) Select one to prioritize. Consider how this chosen activity changes your perspective.

_____

_____

_____

_____

_____

_____

_____

_____

_____

_____

_____

_____

_____

_____

_____

# Day 5

Look up positive affirmations online and select one to place on your bathroom mirror. Recite it aloud every time you visit the bathroom. Evaluate how repeating positive affirmations throughout the day impacts your overall mood and perspective.

_____

_____

_____

_____

_____

_____

_____

_____

_____

_____

_____

_____

_____

_____

_____

_____

_____

# Affirmation 27

# Blame does not hold me back.

As a caregiver, it's quite possible to blame yourself for your kiddo's situation. For example, my daughter was born two months early because I was diagnosed with severe preeclampsia. Her early birth led to a long NICU stay, a feeding tube, and many other difficulties. It's easy for me to think that if I had eaten healthier, exercised more, or managed stress better, I could have prevented her early birth and many of her health difficulties. It's understandable that I get stuck dwelling on "what ifs." But if I stand back and am honest with myself, I didn't choose to get preeclampsia, and I didn't choose for her to go through all of her struggles. Blaming yourself adds a lot of extra weight to your day-to-day life, and being a caregiver already comes with a lot of weight. This week, work on letting go of blame.

# Day 1

Look up the definition of "blame." How can blaming yourself for things out of your control cause more damage than help?

_____

_____

_____

_____

_____

_____

_____

_____

_____

_____

_____

_____

_____

_____

_____

_____

_____

_____

_____

_____

# Day 2

Think of at least one thing that you blame yourself for currently. How would letting go of this blame change your life?

_____

_____

_____

_____

_____

_____

_____

_____

_____

_____

_____

_____

_____

_____

_____

_____

_____

_____

# Day 3

Review your list from Day 2. Make a list of things that are in your control and a list of things that are not in your control as it relates to the situation(s) from Day 2. Compare the lists. How much of the situation was in your control vs. how much was not in your control?

_____

_____

_____

_____

_____

_____

_____

_____

_____

_____

_____

_____

_____

_____

_____

_____

_____

# Day 4

Do you know someone else who blames themselves for something they aren't in control of? How does this blame affect this person? How does acknowledging this effect on the other person change your perspective about blame and/or encourage you to let go of anything you blame yourself for?

_____

_____

_____

_____

_____

_____

_____

_____

_____

_____

_____

_____

_____

_____

_____

_____

# Day 5

Research ways to let go of painful past events. Pick one and let go of something that is weighing you down (for example, write it down and shred/burn it, write it on a helium balloon and let it go, etc.) How do you feel after you complete this activity?

_____

_____

_____

_____

_____

_____

_____

_____

_____

_____

_____

_____

_____

_____

_____

_____

_____

# Affirmation 28

# It is ok for me to feel all varieties of emotions.

It was a groundbreaking realization when someone told me that feelings aren't wrong; it's how we respond to the feelings that matter. Caregiving can be incredibly difficult, and acknowledging the challenges can be looked down upon. But recognizing your feelings helps you live life to the fullest; feelings mean you care. Whether good or bad, feelings are a normal part of life. There is no shame in your feelings.

# __Day 1__

At the end of the day, take a moment to list the different feelings you experienced during the day. Whether positive or negative, write them down and acknowledge how you felt.

_____

_____

_____

_____

_____

_____

_____

_____

_____

_____

_____

_____

_____

_____

_____

_____

_____

_____

# Day 2

We often use the same emotion names such as mad, sad, scared, happy, etc. Look up a feelings wheel. How does seeing more detailed feeling names help you understand and better process your feelings? Make a new list of the feelings you experienced today, but this time, use words from the feelings wheel.

_____

_____

_____

_____

_____

_____

_____

_____

_____

_____

_____

_____

_____

_____

_____

_____

# **Day 3**

Reflect on your happiest or one of your happiest memories. What about this memory made you feel most happy?

_____

_____

_____

_____

_____

_____

_____

_____

_____

_____

_____

_____

_____

_____

_____

_____

_____

_____

_____

_____

# **Day 4**

What was the strongest feeling you experienced today? Why did you feel that way? Take a moment to write down your thoughts. How does writing about feelings affect you?

_____

_____

_____

_____

_____

_____

_____

_____

_____

_____

_____

_____

_____

_____

_____

_____

# Day 5

Make a list of at least three reasons why it is okay for you to embrace your own emotions and why it's okay if your emotions don't match other people's feelings.

_____

_____

_____

_____

_____

_____

_____

_____

_____

_____

_____

_____

_____

_____

_____

_____

_____

_____

# Affirmation 29

# My child has many strengths and gifts.

Sometimes, it's easy to get caught up in what needs improvement and miss the beauty of the person right in front of us. It's important to remember to focus on our child's strengths and talents rather than just their weaknesses. (For example, focusing on a skill that your kiddo is trying to master in a therapy so much that you miss out on the joy they add to the world.) Everyone has things they are good at, and this week, we will focus on looking for strengths.

# Day 1

Write a list of your kiddo's strengths and talents.

# Day 2

Reflect on the list from yesterday and consider how these talents help improve others' lives?

_____

_____

_____

_____

_____

_____

_____

_____

_____

_____

_____

_____

_____

_____

_____

_____

_____

_____

_____

_____

# Day 3

Identify one of your child's strengths that could be improved. What is this attribute, and how can you work on making it stronger?

_____

_____

_____

_____

_____

_____

_____

_____

_____

_____

_____

_____

_____

_____

_____

_____

_____

_____

# Day 4

Avoid the temptation to compare. We look at "normal" kids and sometimes wish that our kids were "normal." Take a few minutes to ponder. Are you comparing your kid to others? If so, how can you stop and just look at them for who they are and their strengths and weaknesses without the comparisons?

_____

_____

_____

_____

_____

_____

_____

_____

_____

_____

_____

_____

_____

_____

_____

# Day 5

Reach out to family, friends, and teachers to ask about your child's biggest strengths. Write these down and compare them to your original list. Do you see the same things in your child that others do?

_____

_____

_____

_____

_____

_____

_____

_____

_____

_____

_____

_____

_____

_____

_____

_____

_____

# **Affirmation 30**

# I create joy.

Looking at endless to-do lists can seem daunting. Planners scheduled with appointment after appointment or procedure after procedure are stressful. It is so easy to get caught up in the stress and overwhelming feelings that we stop enjoying life. We may find it hard to catch our breath or relax. All of these negative emotions can keep us from finding joy in our day-to-day lives. We will focus on creating joy and happiness in these next few activities.

# Day 1

Think about something that brings you happiness. These moments often don't happen by chance; we need to intentionally plan for them in our lives. Today, how can you intentionally incorporate something that brings you joy?

# Day 2

When was the last time you let your guard down and just had some silly fun with your kiddo? We often don't do this enough, but when we do, the laughter and joy shared are priceless. Find a way to have a fun and silly moment with your child today.

_____

_____

_____

_____

_____

_____

_____

_____

_____

_____

_____

_____

_____

_____

_____

# Day 3

For many of us, joy is tied to our favorite foods. Try incorporating one of your favorite foods into your day today. How does purposefully including something that brings you joy affect your day?

_____

_____

_____

_____

_____

_____

_____

_____

_____

_____

_____

_____

_____

_____

_____

_____

_____

# Day 4

What does joy mean to you? Look up the dictionary definition and consider if it matches your definition. What senses are involved when you experience joy? If you had to redefine joy based on your own experiences, what would you write?

_____

_____

_____

_____

_____

_____

_____

_____

_____

_____

_____

_____

_____

_____

_____

_____

# Day 5

Today, intentionally share the joy with someone else. This might involve writing a card or text, sending flowers, or actively supporting someone in need. How does making someone else happy impact your own joy?

_____

_____

_____

_____

_____

_____

_____

_____

_____

_____

_____

_____

_____

_____

_____

_____

_____

_____

# Affirmation 31

# I continue to learn new things.

Being a parent to a child with medical issues has taught me a great deal. It is so important to be open-minded and to look at things from different view points. Being a great caregiver means constantly learning new things. You may not have any formal schooling, but you know your child, their condition, and their needs.

# Day 1

Look up information about your child's condition online. Try to find a new source that you haven't explored before. Did this new source remind you of anything or provide any new information that you were not aware of before?

_____

_____

_____

_____

_____

_____

_____

_____

_____

_____

_____

_____

_____

_____

_____

_____

_____

# **Day 2**

Talk to another parent who has a child with a medical condition or special needs. Ask them if they know of any exceptional healthcare providers, programs, copay assistance programs, etc. Prepare a list of questions and see what you can learn.

_____

_____

_____

_____

_____

_____

_____

_____

_____

_____

_____

_____

_____

_____

_____

_____

_____

# Day 3

Research treatment options for your kiddo's condition. Were there any options that you were unfamiliar with? Look up potential side effects, etc. Use this knowledge, along with the information your doctor has shared, to create an informed opinion.

_____

_____

_____

_____

_____

_____

_____

_____

_____

_____

_____

_____

_____

_____

_____

_____

_____

# Day 4

Have you ever had the feeling that something just isn't right? I have learned to trust my instincts, and you should too. If any symptoms don't seem to make sense, or if you are confused about your child's condition, or if it seems like there might be something else going on in addition to the original diagnosis, do some research and record your observations. Make sure to share it with the doctor at the next appointment.

_____

_____

_____

_____

_____

_____

_____

_____

_____

_____

_____

_____

_____

_____

# Day 5

What is something non-medical that you are curious about? Spend a few minutes researching that today. Write your notes down below.

_____

_____

_____

_____

_____

_____

_____

_____

_____

_____

_____

_____

_____

_____

_____

_____

_____

_____

# Affirmation 32

# Some people won't understand my situation, and that's ok.

As a caregiver, one of the most disheartening things I've encountered is dealing with people who don't understand or refuse to try to understand my situation. It can be difficult for those who aren't caregivers to comprehend the challenges I face because things in my day-to-day life are not even in their frames of reference. Coming to terms with their lack of understanding and realizing that it doesn't define me or change my circumstances is empowering.

# Day 1

Take a few minutes to research what it means to set boundaries. Who is someone that you feel doesn't understand your situation? How could you set boundaries, limit contact time, or explain (if possible) what your life is like to this person to help them better understand your point of view?

---

# Day 2

How do you feel when someone isn't understanding of your situation? Make a list of these feelings. What can you tell yourself when these feelings start to creep in so they don't overcome you? Come up with a positive phrase that you can repeat to yourself when these feelings arise.

_____

_____

_____

_____

_____

_____

_____

_____

_____

_____

_____

_____

_____

_____

_____

_____

# Day 3

What is a medical condition you know very little or nothing about? Take a few minutes to research that condition today. How does learning about this condition help you be able to understand another caregiver who works with a similar situation?

_____

_____

_____

_____

_____

_____

_____

_____

_____

_____

_____

_____

_____

_____

_____

_____

_____

_____

# Day 4

Make a list of people whom you can trust and talk to about your caregiving experience. These individuals should be empathetic, good listeners, and should not have unrealistic expectations of you. Keep this list handy for times when someone doesn't understand so you have a support system you can reach out to that gets it.

_____

_____

_____

_____

_____

_____

_____

_____

_____

_____

_____

_____

_____

_____

_____

# Day 5

What is the most harmful or hurtful thing that non-understanding people do? Do they place unrealistic expectations on you or do they demand more than you are capable of giving? Prepare a response for such situations and keep it in mind for when you need it.

_____

_____

_____

_____

_____

_____

_____

_____

_____

_____

_____

_____

_____

_____

_____

_____

# Affirmation 33

# My life is unique.

We often use the word "normal" to label things, but I believe it simply reflects individual expectations. Since we're all different, our expectations will naturally vary. Having taught elementary school for years, I'm not convinced that "normal" truly exists. We are all unique individuals with our own strengths, weaknesses, differences, and life challenges. Everyone has a unique situation, including caregivers. After returning from Mayo Clinic with my oldest daughter, a colleague asked if I planned on having more kids. She then mentioned that kids aren't typically as difficult as my daughter. While the kids in her family didn't have complex medical needs, her situation is just as unique as yours and mine, I just don't know the details.

# Day 1

Look up the definition of "normal" online. How would you describe what society says is "normal" about raising kids?

_____

_____

_____

_____

_____

_____

_____

_____

_____

_____

_____

_____

_____

_____

_____

_____

_____

_____

# **Day 2**

Write about your family's "normal" for a few minutes. How does your "normal" differ from society's "normal" that you wrote about yesterday?

_____

_____

_____

_____

_____

_____

_____

_____

_____

_____

_____

_____

_____

_____

_____

_____

_____

# Day 3

When have you expected something to be "normal?" Did this thing turn out as you planned? If so, is it good that it was "normal?" If it didn't, did it turn out better or worse than you imagined?

_____

_____

_____

_____

_____

_____

_____

_____

_____

_____

_____

_____

_____

_____

_____

_____

_____

_____

# Day 4

Are there any benefits to other people believing that your life is "normal," like theirs? How does it make you feel when other people don't seem to understand the uniqueness of your situation?

_____

_____

_____

_____

_____

_____

_____

_____

_____

_____

_____

_____

_____

_____

_____

_____

# Day 5

Moving forward, how can you keep yourself from assuming that other people and their families are "normal?" How will changing your mindset help you in the future?

_____

_____

_____

_____

_____

_____

_____

_____

_____

_____

_____

_____

_____

_____

_____

_____

_____

_____

# Affirmation 34

# I have needs, and they matter.

As a caregiver, I caught myself prioritizing the needs of my child and neglecting my own well-being. Yes, there are non-negotiable things that have to be done each day, but that doesn't mean I shouldn't add self-care to that list of non-negotiables. While focusing on caregiving is important, it's crucial to take care of yourself as well to prevent burnout and additional challenges.

# Day 1

Identify one daily self-care activity, such as taking a shower or reading a book, and prioritize it today. Reflect on how making this activity a priority makes you feel.

_____

_____

_____

_____

_____

_____

_____

_____

_____

_____

_____

_____

_____

_____

_____

_____

_____

_____

# Day 2

Create a list of at least five essential self-care activities. If it's not feasible to do them all daily, schedule them on a weekly basis and make them non-negotiable by blocking out time on your calendar for each activity.

_____

_____

_____

_____

_____

_____

_____

_____

_____

_____

_____

_____

_____

_____

_____

# **Day 3**

Many times, it's easy to forget about our emotional needs. It's easy to say we need to get dressed for the day, do our hair, etc. Today, ponder about what emotional need you currently have. Schedule at least 5 minutes today to address this emotional need.

_____

_____

_____

_____

_____

_____

_____

_____

_____

_____

_____

_____

_____

_____

_____

_____

_____

# Day 4

Look up "Maslow's Hierarchy of Needs" online. What did you learn? What level of Maslow's pyramid are you currently at?

_____

_____

_____

_____

_____

_____

_____

_____

_____

_____

_____

_____

_____

_____

_____

_____

# Day 5

Based on your research from yesterday, brainstorm a plan to ensure that you're not just surviving but thriving. What small actions could you take each day to ensure you flourish?

_____

_____

_____

_____

_____

_____

_____

_____

_____

_____

_____

_____

_____

_____

_____

_____

_____

_____

# Affirmation 35

# I speak up.

Throughout the caregiving journey, it can feel like you have very little control over important things such as insurance authorizations, getting medications covered, and even something as simple as getting your child to see the correct specialist. By speaking up, you can take control.

# **Day 1**

Think about a time when you were told something couldn't happen (medically related or not). Did you speak up and advocate for yourself and your child? If not, how can you make a plan to speak up next time you are in a similar situation?

_____

_____

_____

_____

_____

_____

_____

_____

_____

_____

_____

_____

_____

_____

_____

_____

# Day 2

We often hear about a parent's instincts. It can be hard to trust those instincts, especially if you don't have a medical background and research to back your instincts. What is an instinct you recently had about your child's care? Did you express this instinct? If you did not, make a plan to bring up your thoughts at the next available opportunity.

_____

_____

_____

_____

_____

_____

_____

_____

_____

_____

_____

_____

_____

_____

_____

# Day 3

Think about a time in your life when you stood up for something you believed in. How did taking a stand make you feel? How can looking at this past example help you continue to stand up and speak up, especially in the caregiver setting?

_____

_____

_____

_____

_____

_____

_____

_____

_____

_____

_____

_____

_____

_____

_____

_____

_____

# Day 4

It is very easy to associate the words "speak up" with contention. Write down a nice way to express your thoughts that allows you to advocate and treat others respectfully.

_____

_____

_____

_____

_____

_____

_____

_____

_____

_____

_____

_____

_____

_____

_____

_____

_____

# Day 5

Who is someone in your life or a role model who speaks up on a regular basis? What makes him/her successful when speaking up? What part of their success can you apply to your life?

_____

_____

_____

_____

_____

_____

_____

_____

_____

_____

_____

_____

_____

_____

_____

_____

_____

_____

# Affirmation 36

# I find a good team of doctors and professionals.

In sports, we hear about "dream teams," teams that have a fantastic set of players who know how to use each person's strengths to make the whole team stronger. This week, we will focus on creating a "dream team" of doctors and professionals for your kids.

# Day 1

Write down your child's current medical team. Do you feel like your child has a "dream team?" Do each of the team members listen to you and treat you and your child with respect?

_____

_____

_____

_____

_____

_____

_____

_____

_____

_____

_____

_____

_____

_____

_____

_____

_____

_____

# Day 2

Identify if there is a professional on the list from Day 1 who doesn't fit into your child's "dream team." Seek recommendations for a replacement provider.

_____

_____

_____

_____

_____

_____

_____

_____

_____

_____

_____

_____

_____

_____

_____

_____

_____

# Day 3

If you could create the perfect doctor or professional to join your child's team, what characteristics are must-haves on your list?

_____

_____

_____

_____

_____

_____

_____

_____

_____

_____

_____

_____

_____

_____

_____

_____

_____

_____

_____

_____

# __Day 4__

Look back at your list on Day 3 and make a list of characteristics that you absolutely do not want a professional on your child's medical team to have.

_____

_____

_____

_____

_____

_____

_____

_____

_____

_____

_____

_____

_____

_____

_____

_____

_____

# Day 5

Review your lists from the last two days. Reflect on your child's medical teams and see if any insights or realizations emerge that can help you make important changes and/or validate your selection of providers.

_____

_____

_____

_____

_____

_____

_____

_____

_____

_____

_____

_____

_____

_____

_____

_____

# Affirmation 37

# I am talented.

It can be so effortless to forget about yourself, your talents, likes, and dislikes. But losing yourself can cause additional struggles. Remember to focus on your strengths.

# **Day 1**

Make a list of at least five things that you are good at. Write down the last time that you did each thing. Has it been a long time or were you able to do this thing recently? How does it make you feel when you complete these activities?

_____

_____

_____

_____

_____

_____

_____

_____

_____

_____

_____

_____

_____

_____

_____

_____

_____

# Day 2

Pick one thing from your list of talents, and make sure to spend five or ten minutes doing that activity today. How do you feel after spending time on something you are passionate about?

_____

_____

_____

_____

_____

_____

_____

_____

_____

_____

_____

_____

_____

_____

_____

# Day 3

Often it is straightforward to think of talents as visible things: the ability to play an instrument, being good at a sport, getting good grades, and more. But there are so many more hidden talents that are quiet, less noticeable, and also important beyond measure! What are some of your hidden talents that help you as a caregiver? (Examples: kind, loving, empathetic, good listener, creative, etc.)

_____

_____

_____

_____

_____

_____

_____

_____

_____

_____

_____

_____

_____

_____

# Day 4

What is a hobby or activity you have always wanted to try but never had the chance to do? Make a little bit of time this week to try out one of these things. Could this thing become a new talent? Can it be a tool you add to your arsenal to stay strong and positive?

_____

_____

_____

_____

_____

_____

_____

_____

_____

_____

_____

_____

_____

_____

_____

# Day 5

Do you feel talented right now? If so, what is instilling confidence in yourself? If not, what makes you feel not gifted? Write down how you can continue to feel talented or how you can work to start feeling talented.

_____

_____

_____

_____

_____

_____

_____

_____

_____

_____

_____

_____

_____

_____

_____

_____

_____

# Affirmation 38

# I have hope.

Sometimes, hope seems nonexistent. It can feel like you're on a train traveling through a dark tunnel, but you have no idea where you're going, how much farther there is to go, or if the tunnel will end. In caregiving, you have to make sure that you can constantly look for and see the light at the end of the tunnel. This light at the end of the tunnel is hope, a feeling that helps us continue to move forward.

# Day 1

Look up the definition of "hope" on the internet and make a list of the things that you are hoping for most right now.

_____

_____

_____

_____

_____

_____

_____

_____

_____

_____

_____

_____

_____

_____

_____

_____

_____

_____

# Day 2

What are some images and symbols that represent hope? Explain why these images and symbols are good representations of hope.

_____

_____

_____

_____

_____

_____

_____

_____

_____

_____

_____

_____

_____

_____

_____

# Day 3

In caregiving, many things are often out of your control. Reflect on how you can continue to have hope even when you aren't in control.

_____

_____

_____

_____

_____

_____

_____

_____

_____

_____

_____

_____

_____

_____

_____

_____

_____

_____

# Day 4

Think of something small that you could place on your bathroom mirror, your car, or somewhere else that you will see often to remind yourself to have hope. Put this small reminder in a place where you will see it multiple times a day.

_____

_____

_____

_____

_____

_____

_____

_____

_____

_____

_____

_____

_____

_____

_____

# **Day 5**

Recall a time when you thought there was no hope, but things ended up turning out well. Reflect on how you can hold on to this experience when things look dark in the future. Also, consider if there are any other experiences like this one that you can use to anchor yourself.

_____

_____

_____

_____

_____

_____

_____

_____

_____

_____

_____

_____

_____

_____

_____

_____

# Affirmation 39

# I use available resources.

There are many resources to assist you and your kiddo in your journey! It has taken me many years to learn about these resources, and I still discover new ones that improve our lives on a regular basis. What new resources will you discover this week?

# Day 1

List the resources you are currently using to make your life easier. Reflect on how your situation would be different without these supports.

_____

_____

_____

_____

_____

_____

_____

_____

_____

_____

_____

_____

_____

_____

_____

_____

_____

# __Day 2__

Make a list of things you currently need help with or support you need in your caregiving journey (e.g., support groups, financial assistance, copay assistance programs for medications, Medicaid waivers). Highlight the items you need the most.

_____

_____

_____

_____

_____

_____

_____

_____

_____

_____

_____

_____

_____

_____

_____

_____

# Day 3

Ask a doctor on your kiddo's medical team for a social worker's phone number. Call the number and ask the social worker for a list of different available support options.

_____

_____

_____

_____

_____

_____

_____

_____

_____

_____

_____

_____

_____

_____

_____

_____

_____

_____

# Day 4

Research one of the supports that the social worker shared with you. Determine if this support will provide help. If it doesn't work for your family, find another support that does.

_____

_____

_____

_____

_____

_____

_____

_____

_____

_____

_____

_____

_____

_____

_____

_____

_____

_____

# Day 5

Check the income guidelines for Medicaid, your state's child healthcare plan, and WIC. See if your family qualifies for any of these supports.

_____

_____

_____

_____

_____

_____

_____

_____

_____

_____

_____

_____

_____

_____

_____

_____

_____

_____

# Affirmation 40

# I am vulnerable.

There is a lot of pressure these days to say things perfectly. Feelings, concerns, and even being human are messy. Even though your thoughts, feelings, and concerns are not perfect, it is important to share them honestly, as solutions can't be discovered without the problem being brought to the drawing board.

# Day 1

What is your natural inclination (fight, flight, freeze) when you get nervous, scared, or even disagree with someone? How does this response affect your ability to be a caregiver?

_____

_____

_____

_____

_____

_____

_____

_____

_____

_____

_____

_____

_____

_____

_____

_____

_____

# Day 2

What is something that is worrying you that you haven't shared with anyone? Communicate this thing that is weighing you down with someone today. How did sharing change your feelings?

_____

_____

_____

_____

_____

_____

_____

_____

_____

_____

_____

_____

_____

_____

_____

_____

# Day 3

Think back to a doctor's appointment or conversation with a medical professional in which you didn't share your feelings, concerns, questions, etc. What emotions prevented you from speaking honestly? How does acknowledging and labeling these feelings help you move on and improve your communication with medical professionals in the future?

_____

_____

_____

_____

_____

_____

_____

_____

_____

_____

_____

_____

_____

_____

# Day 4

What are some fears that you have about being vulnerable? How can you overcome these fears and become better at advocating for yourself?

_____

_____

_____

_____

_____

_____

_____

_____

_____

_____

_____

_____

_____

_____

_____

_____

# Day 5

As caregivers, we try and teach our kids to speak up. We want them to tell us if something is wrong, if something hurts, the best part of their day, etc. How will your setting an example of speaking up/being vulnerable help your child learn to do the same thing?

_____

_____

_____

_____

_____

_____

_____

_____

_____

_____

_____

_____

_____

_____

_____

_____

# Affirmation 41

# I am firm like a rock.

When you think of the word "rock," what are the first words that come to mind? How does a rock relate to stability? Becoming a figurative rock will help you better handle the unknown challenges with caregiving.

# Day 1

Look up the definition of the word "stable." What are some things in nature that don't move despite bad weather and other negative influences? What do these things have in common, or what characteristics allow them to be stable?

_____

_____

_____

_____

_____

_____

_____

_____

_____

_____

_____

_____

_____

_____

_____

_____

_____

# Day 2

Select something that you listed as stable in nature yesterday. How can you apply some of the same principles to your life? How will these principles help you in figurative times of bad weather?

_____

_____

_____

_____

_____

_____

_____

_____

_____

_____

_____

_____

_____

_____

_____

_____

_____

# Day 3

Think of some things in nature that are unstable. What are the characteristics of these unstable parts of nature? How can you avoid the things that cause instability?

_____

_____

_____

_____

_____

_____

_____

_____

_____

_____

_____

_____

_____

_____

_____

_____

# **Day 4**

A tree's branches sway in the wind, while the roots are immoveable. How does this analogy apply to your life and the medical challenges that arise?

_____

_____

_____

_____

_____

_____

_____

_____

_____

_____

_____

_____

_____

_____

_____

_____

# Day 5

What do tree roots need to become strong and healthy? What do you need in your life to be stable? How can you make these things a priority?

_____

_____

_____

_____

_____

_____

_____

_____

_____

_____

_____

_____

_____

_____

_____

_____

_____

_____

# Affirmation 42

# I can find gifts (positives) in each day.

Good things happen each day, but it can be difficult to see them when we're buried in the hard. Making a point to acknowledge the positive can increase the color and joy in our lives while preventing us from feeling mundane and stuck.

# Day 1

What is your favorite gift you received? What made it your favorite gift? Look up the definition of the word "gift." Why is it important to realize that there are no strings attached to true gifts?

_____

_____

_____

_____

_____

_____

_____

_____

_____

_____

_____

_____

_____

_____

_____

_____

_____

# Day 2

How does it make you feel when you are given a thoughtful gift? What would happen if you labeled good things that happened to you during the day as gifts?

_____

_____

_____

_____

_____

_____

_____

_____

_____

_____

_____

_____

_____

_____

_____

_____

_____

# Day 3

Make a list of the good things that happen today.

_____

_____

_____

_____

_____

_____

_____

_____

_____

_____

_____

_____

_____

_____

_____

_____

_____

_____

# Day 4

Think of something unexpected that happened in your day. Maybe you were late to an event, ruined a new recipe, or left the milk out of the fridge. How can you reframe this situation and find something positive about it? (For example, my daughter was almost late to school because I lost track of time, but we were busy spending some positive one-on-one time together, which was more important to her than a tardy.) Could this unexpected part of your day be labeled as a gift?

_____

_____

_____

_____

_____

_____

_____

_____

_____

_____

_____

_____

# Day 5

Make a list of all the gifts you receive from people today. These gifts can include anything from someone smiling at you to someone letting you go before them in the grocery line. How does writing down these gifts make you feel about your day?

_____

_____

_____

_____

_____

_____

_____

_____

_____

_____

_____

_____

_____

_____

_____

_____

_____

# Affirmation 43

# I know when to slow down and/or ask for assistance.

Our body tries to warn us before we are burnt out. Once we recognize these signs in our body, we should try to do things differently (slow down and/or ask for help) to prevent complete burnout. Sometimes, it can be hard to admit that we need help, but acknowledging your struggles and making positive changes will benefit your whole family!

# Day 1

Think back to several times that you were burnt out. What are some of the warnings, feelings, or even physical symptoms that came before the burnout?

_____

_____

_____

_____

_____

_____

_____

_____

_____

_____

_____

_____

_____

_____

_____

_____

_____

# Day 2

When you start getting the pre burn-out feelings and/or physical symptoms, create a plan to help you slow down before things get worse. (Some examples include taking a day off from appointments, crossing unessential things off your schedule, etc.)

_____

_____

_____

_____

_____

_____

_____

_____

_____

_____

_____

_____

_____

_____

_____

# Day 3

As caregivers, we are prone to feel isolated and alone, but we do best when we have people around supporting us. Make a list of at least three people that you know you can ask for help and count on when you need it.

_____

_____

_____

_____

_____

_____

_____

_____

_____

_____

_____

_____

_____

_____

_____

_____

# **Day 4**

What are some things that make your to-do list seem overwhelming? How can you pass some of these tasks on to a support person, set them aside to complete a different day, or make them a family affair? Refer to the list of support people you made yesterday and think about who could best offer the assistance you need in different scenarios or how your family can work together to reduce the load on your plate.

_____

_____

_____

_____

_____

_____

_____

_____

_____

_____

_____

_____

_____

_____

# Day 5

Asking for help can be difficult. We see that other people are busy, work, etc., and the list of reasons not to ask someone for help can go on and on. What are some feelings that prevent you from asking for help? How can you challenge these feelings?

_____

_____

_____

_____

_____

_____

_____

_____

_____

_____

_____

_____

_____

_____

_____

_____

_____

# Affirmation 44

# My world is

# colorful.

Colors add so much detail to our worlds! I am spoiled and have such a hard time watching black-and-white movies because they don't have color. The movie can be amazing, but if it's in black and white, I often don't even give it a chance! I like color. Sometimes, as a caregiver, we can get stuck in what seems like the black-and-white, sometimes gray, the mundane, and unexciting. Keep looking for color! That's what makes this world more palatable!

# Day 1

What is your favorite color? Acknowledge every time you see that color today. Where did you see it? How did looking for that color affect your day?

_____

_____

_____

_____

_____

_____

_____

_____

_____

_____

_____

_____

_____

_____

_____

_____

_____

# Day 2

What does color do for your life? Does it have any effect on your mood? What if everything was black-and-white?

_____

_____

_____

_____

_____

_____

_____

_____

_____

_____

_____

_____

_____

_____

_____

_____

_____

# Day 3

Color is something we see, but other things can also be referred to as "colorful." Look up the definition of "colorful." What is your version of a colorful world?

_____

_____

_____

_____

_____

_____

_____

_____

_____

_____

_____

_____

_____

_____

_____

_____

_____

# Day 4

What is your kiddo's favorite color? Help your child play "I Spy" and look for everything that is their favorite color today. How did this task give you a positive focus for the day? How did it affect your interactions with your child?

_____

_____

_____

_____

_____

_____

_____

_____

_____

_____

_____

_____

_____

_____

_____

_____

# Day 5

Art is a fun way to acknowledge and share the beauty of colors. Do a simple art project with your child today. Make sure to include each person's favorite colors.

_____

_____

_____

_____

_____

_____

_____

_____

_____

_____

_____

_____

_____

_____

_____

_____

_____

_____

# Affirmation 45

# I live in a medically advanced time period.

Medical advancements are constant and give us options and hope for our kiddos. Years ago, many conditions that are treated today were unnamed, which also meant they were without treatment. Just having the ability to name a diagnosis helps us feel like we have some power over our child's condition and allows us to make decisions for the best types of care.

# Day 1

Make a list of your child's current medications, treatments, etc. Put a star by ones that weren't around 100 years ago. Underline the medication, treatment, etc., that you are most grateful for right now.

_____

_____

_____

_____

_____

_____

_____

_____

_____

_____

_____

_____

_____

_____

_____

_____

_____

_____

# Day 2

Doctors and scientists are continually learning new things, developing new treatments, and more. Most of these medical advancements can be found in medical articles or research papers. What is something you would like a better understanding of about your child's condition and/or treatment options? Spend a few minutes today researching this condition and/or treatment options. What did you learn? How doable or accessible is the treatment?

_____

_____

_____

_____

_____

_____

_____

_____

_____

_____

_____

_____

_____

_____

# Day 3

Are the doctors and medical professionals on your child's team eager and ready to learn more about current medical advancements or are they stuck in the knowledge of how things worked from years ago? Do they share updated research with you? How do their viewpoints affect your child's care?

_____

_____

_____

_____

_____

_____

_____

_____

_____

_____

_____

_____

_____

_____

_____

_____

# Day 4

How does having a positive attitude towards continued growth and learning help encourage medical advancements? Are all medical advancements good? Form your own opinion using medical research.

_____

_____

_____

_____

_____

_____

_____

_____

_____

_____

_____

_____

_____

_____

_____

_____

# Day 5

What single treatment, diagnosis, etc., a result of continuing medical research and study, has helped make your journey as a caregiver easier? What would your life be like without this knowledge?

_____

_____

_____

_____

_____

_____

_____

_____

_____

_____

_____

_____

_____

_____

_____

_____

# Affirmation 46

# I prioritize mental health.

Mental health is a topic that is often avoided because it can be uncomfortable. In the mental health trainings I took as a teacher, it was always the case that having a hard conversation about mental health was better than avoiding it. I have seen the same principle ring true in my life. My mental health is better when I focus on it and do things to keep it well-oiled and functioning.

# Day 1

Rate your mental health on a scale of 1-10 (10 being amazing, and 1 being that you're really struggling.) Why did you rank your mental health at this level? If it is low, what needs to change? Brainstorm some ways you could increase your rating. If it is already at a good level, list some ways you can maintain this level.

_____

_____

_____

_____

_____

_____

_____

_____

_____

_____

_____

_____

_____

_____

_____

_____

# Day 2

Rate your kiddo's mental health on a scale of 1-10. What can you do to help increase their ranking or ensure it stays near a score of 10?

_____

_____

_____

_____

_____

_____

_____

_____

_____

_____

_____

_____

_____

_____

_____

_____

# Day 3

Make a list of at least five mental health supports. If you can't think of many, look up some ideas online. Put a star by the support you are most likely to use.

_____

_____

_____

_____

_____

_____

_____

_____

_____

_____

_____

_____

_____

_____

_____

_____

_____

# Day 4

Dismissing thoughts about mental health, especially if you are on the verge of a breakdown, can be tempting. For some reason, it can appear that if we push feelings/thoughts aside and/or don't acknowledge them, the thing/thoughts, etc., aren't actually there. Why is it important to be cognizant of your and your family's mental health?

_____

_____

_____

_____

_____

_____

_____

_____

_____

_____

_____

_____

_____

_____

# **Day 5**

Do you feel like you could ever ask someone for help with your mental health if needed? Why do you feel you could or couldn't ask for help? If needed, find the courage to take the first step to increase your mental health.

_____

_____

_____

_____

_____

_____

_____

_____

_____

_____

_____

_____

_____

_____

_____

_____

_____

# Affirmation 47

# I can make any environment feel like home.

As a caregiver, it is common to spend lots of time away from home, either at doctor's appointments, therapy appointments, hospital stays, surgery centers, and many more locations. Often, these places are very business-like, bland, and uninviting. You may feel like you are never home. This week, we will gear up to change that and focus on making wherever we feel like home.

# Day 1

Where are you spending most of your time? Do these places offer a cozy, warm vibe, or do they feel strict, formal, and business-like?

_____

_____

_____

_____

_____

_____

_____

_____

_____

_____

_____

_____

_____

_____

_____

_____

_____

_____

# Day 2

Think about what makes your home different from the doctor's office. For kids, home is often a place that is comfortable and has their favorite toys. Assemble a doctor's office bag that has fun activities that you can bring to help your child feel at home while away from home. Include games, tangrams, coloring books, supplies, a favorite stuffed animal, etc. Only use this bag at doctors' appointments so your kiddo doesn't get bored quickly with the items inside.

# Day 3

Where is a place that you spend a lot of time that feels uncomfortable or that could just feel warmer? What could you do to that space to increase the warmth and liven it up? (Hang decorations, bring activities and snacks with you, invite a friend, etc.)

_____

_____

_____

_____

_____

_____

_____

_____

_____

_____

_____

_____

_____

_____

_____

_____

# Day 4

Home is associated with people. Who can you invite to come sit with you at an appointment or visit with you after the appointment, treatment, or surgery so you still have people around you no matter your location? Having support can help any environment feel more like home.

_____

_____

_____

_____

_____

_____

_____

_____

_____

_____

_____

_____

_____

_____

_____

_____

# **Day 5**

What is one thing in your life that gets forgotten or pushed to the back burner when medical appointments or procedures become the priority? (Ex. I love listening to music but find that when I'm busy, I forget to turn it on.) How could you incorporate this thing into your daily life even when you aren't home?

_____

_____

_____

_____

_____

_____

_____

_____

_____

_____

_____

_____

_____

_____

_____

_____

_____

# Affirmation 48

# I can find comfort.

All children love comfort items! These items can be stuffed animals, a special blanket, a binkie, and the list could continue. As we grow up, it's easy to push aside our comfort items because we are getting "too old" for them. But adults too, can find comfort in little, simple things just like the young ones do.

# Day 1

What is your child's comfort item? What is it about that item that makes it a thing of comfort and ease? Make a list of adjectives that describe why your kiddo finds this item comforting.

_____

_____

_____

_____

_____

_____

_____

_____

_____

_____

_____

_____

_____

_____

_____

_____

_____

# Day 2

List five things that bring you comfort. Why do these things bring you comfort?

_____

_____

_____

_____

_____

_____

_____

_____

_____

_____

_____

_____

_____

_____

_____

_____

_____

_____

# Day 3

Pick something from your list yesterday and do it/use it today. How did making this comfort item a part of your day change your day for the better?

_____

_____

_____

_____

_____

_____

_____

_____

_____

_____

_____

_____

_____

_____

_____

_____

_____

# Day 4

Pick another comfort thing from your list from Day 2 and do it/use it today. How did making this comfort item a part of your day change your day for the better?

_____

_____

_____

_____

_____

_____

_____

_____

_____

_____

_____

_____

_____

_____

_____

# Day 5

Pick a third comfort item from your list on Day 2 and do it/use it today. How did making this comfort item a part of your day change your day for the better? Which comfort item or practice helped you relax the most out of the strategies you tried this week?

_____

_____

_____

_____

_____

_____

_____

_____

_____

_____

_____

_____

_____

_____

_____

_____

_____

# Affirmation 49

# I love being a parent.

Being a parent is hard work! MIGHTY HARD, to say it right. There is no way to sugarcoat it! In our society, often things that are hard or require work and effort are looked down upon. But there is beauty in the hard! Furthermore, I love seeing experiences through my kids' eyes. They enjoy the simple things and truly enjoy life.

# Day 1

Make a list of at least five favorite family memories. Why did these memories make it to the top of your list? How do these memories remind you of and increase your love for parenting?

_____

_____

_____

_____

_____

_____

_____

_____

_____

_____

_____

_____

_____

_____

_____

_____

_____

_____

# Day 2

Make a list of things that you love about being a parent and another list of things that you don't like. How can you increase the aspects of parenting you love while decreasing or managing the aspects of parenting that aren't your favorite?

_____

_____

_____

_____

_____

_____

_____

_____

_____

_____

_____

_____

_____

_____

_____

_____

# Day 3

Plan an activity that will allow you to make a new positive memory with your family. It can be something simple, like going to play at the park, a picnic, going to the movies, etc. How did you and the rest of your family feel after doing this activity?

_____

_____

_____

_____

_____

_____

_____

_____

_____

_____

_____

_____

_____

_____

_____

_____

# Day 4

List a few of your favorite things in life. (Ex. favorite candy, food, sport, activity, car, etc.) Ponder for a few minutes about why you love these things. How can you incorporate your favorite things into your caregiving journey?

_____

_____

_____

_____

_____

_____

_____

_____

_____

_____

_____

_____

_____

_____

_____

# **Day 5**

Look at your list from Day 1. Pick one of your favorite memories, and come up with a way to memorialize it. (Example: make a picture book, make a memory box, make a slideshow, etc.) On hard days, remind yourself of this positive memory and how much you loved being a parent this day!

_____

_____

_____

_____

_____

_____

_____

_____

_____

_____

_____

_____

_____

_____

_____

_____

# Affirmation 50

# I can zoom out and see the big picture.

Caregiving often requires me to zoom in and focus on specific details. What time is this doctor's appointment, what time does the next medication need to be given, what is causing my child's health problems? Zooming in and trying to answer these questions in detail can be very healthy, help solve problems, and allow you to put together the best, most effective treatment plans. On the flip side, zooming in can keep us from seeing the big picture. Without seeing the overall view, we may miss out on some important details.

# Day 1

Make a list of long-term goals for your family. Have any of these goals been on your radar, or have they been pushed aside due to zooming in?

_____

_____

_____

_____

_____

_____

_____

_____

_____

_____

_____

_____

_____

_____

_____

_____

_____

# Day 2

Look online or on your phone for a picture. Look at it in its original size; now zoom in. What differences do you see? When you zoom in, what finer details become more apparent? What do you miss out on when you stay zoomed in?

_____

_____

_____

_____

_____

_____

_____

_____

_____

_____

_____

_____

_____

_____

_____

_____

# Day 3

It is so easy to get stuck in the zoomed-in phase that we forget to zoom back out. Zoom out now. Why is zooming out an important skill for caregivers?

_____

_____

_____

_____

_____

_____

_____

_____

_____

_____

_____

_____

_____

_____

_____

_____

# Day 4

What tools can help you see something closer up vs. farther away? When using these tools, is it helpful to see the object from both perspectives? Why would seeing the surrounding environment of an object be helpful in the decision-making process? (For example, if you only zoom in to see a bird with binoculars, you will miss seeing the habitat it needs to survive.)

_____

_____

_____

_____

_____

_____

_____

_____

_____

_____

_____

_____

_____

_____

# Day 5

How can zooming out help your family as a whole right now?

_____

_____

_____

_____

_____

_____

_____

_____

_____

_____

_____

_____

_____

_____

_____

_____

_____

_____

_____

_____

_____

# Affirmation 51

_____

_____

_____

_____

Affirmation 51 is left blank so you can create your own. What is something you need a reminder of or something that you are struggling with that an affirmation could help you overcome? What research and/or activities could you complete daily to help you internalize this affirmation?

# Day 1

# Day 2

# Day 3

# Day 4

# Day 5